Modern Wonders Of The World 1

BEIJING AND THE GREAT WALL OF CHINA

Around The World with Jet Lag Jerry 1

Gerald Hansen

Mint Books
New York

While every precaution has been taken in the preparation of this book, the publisher assumes no responsibility for errors or omissions, or for damages resulting from the use of the information contained within.

BEIJING AND THE GREAT WALL OF CHINA: MODERN WONDERS OF THE WORLD 1

First edition. November 30, 2017.
Copyright © 2017 Gerald Hansen.

Written by Gerald Hansen.

Also by Gerald Hansen

The Irish Lottery Series (Fiction):
An Embarrassment of Riches
Hand In The Till
Fleeing The Jurisdiction
Best Served Frozen
Static Cling
Table For Nine At Kebabalicious: A Short Story

Emergency Exit

Jet Lag Jerry Series:
Modern Wonders of the World 2: Peru and Machu Picchu

To Lawrence, Tina and Taal.
Thank you so much for a fantastic time!

ACKNOWLEDGMENTS

Thanks so much to Michael Kiss and Lily Washburn, who gave me the idea for this series. Also, thanks to Yu Guo for help verifying some of the Beijing information. Maddie, I could never write a book without you! Thanks again for your invaluable advice. Fercho, I'm happy we met, and thanks for the inspiration. To Bonita, Ellen, Noam, Estee, Liz and Alysha, thanks for giving me the time off, time after time! And, of course, I'm grateful to all my readers. I hope you enjoy this new series.

JET LAG JERRY TAKES OFF:

ABOUT THIS SERIES

BEIJING AND THE GREAT WALL OF CHINA:

As a Navy brat, I grew up all over the world. I started elementary school in Thailand, graduated high school in Iceland, started working in London, and, after a few gap years too many, I went to college in Ireland. In between, my family and I lived in Northern Ireland, Stuttgart, Germany, and California (twice). I also somehow lived in Berlin for three years. Since then, I've settled in New York City.

I thought my life traveling was over, and counted myself lucky enough to have seen more of the world than most people dream of. But that was before, through the kindness and extreme generosity of a very good friend, I was given a special secret perk in November 2011 that changed my life. It allowed me to travel wherever in our wonderful world I wanted to go. I realized then my traveling had only begun.

I'd already been to most of the European countries. Well, the Western ones, anyway. When I was a child, the Iron Curtain still existed, so Eastern Europe, communist countries that no longer exist like Czechoslovakia and Yugoslavia, but also those that are still there like Romania, Hungary, Poland, etc., were off limits. I think, pre-Berlin Wall fall, they were hardly must-see tourist destinations anyway.

From Ireland, London and especially Germany, it's easy to jump from one country to another as they are all a quick, cheap flight or shortish car drive away (Iceland, not so much). Living in Europe, it was easy for my dad to pile us kids, often grumbling and surly, into the car to drive off to a thrilling new country for the weekend. Our family photos albums, our slides, are packed of the family posing in, sheepish grins under our acne in Belgium, Switzerland, Spain, the Netherlands, France, Scotland, Wales and Austria. When I moved to New York, perched as it is on the northern edge of the Atlantic Ocean, only water stretching out in one direction and endless miles of the US in the other, it hit me that it's a bit more difficult to visit the rest of the world from there.

My New York friends Stacey and Shaun once took a vacation to Morocco, and as I flipped through photos of them riding camels in the desert, as I walked on the exotic carpets they had brought back, I was envious. I'd never be able to afford to go there, I thought. Or, maybe I could, but I'd have to tighten my belt and save up, survive on Top Ramen noodles for months on end to be able to buy the plane ticket, and then there was the cost of the hotel to think of also. It would be near impossible to visit exciting new countries. I had had a lucky childhood, and now it was time to stay in New York. How wrong I was! Thanks to my secret perk, I now had the chance to see and experience some of the other continents, places my paychecks would never allow me access to. So I searched through drawers and boxes and located my long-forgotten passports (with an Irish mother, I'm lucky—again!—to have two), blew the dust off them, realized they had both expired, quickly renewed them, bought a new carry on on sale at Burlington Coat Factory and set off to see the world. It was the birth of Jet Set Jerry. Or so I thought.

I don't know about you, but I'm not independently wealthy, a man of leisure. I can't just tell my boss I'm taking off for a three- or seven-month trip around the world. How would I be able to pay my bills and rent? And I can't afford five- or four- or even three- or even two-star hotels for trip after trip after trip. Somehow, partly from my career as an ESL teacher (English as a Second Language, for adults) at the Manhattan Language school, partly from my international upbringing, and partly from chance due to the cosmopolitan nature of

New York City, I had friends all over the world. From the four corners they had all asked me if I would visit them. "Maybe," I had always answered with a wistful sigh, realizing that the "maybe" was really a "no." But now that "no" was a "yes, indeed! I'll pack right now!"

I figured out that, to see most of my friends, and to visit each of the places, I should follow the three day rule for fish and guests. Both begin to smell after that. So every trip to wherever, near or far, should be three days or less. Really, though, that would be five days, as one day is spent flying somewhere, and another flying back. I wrote emails, messages on Facebook. "Remember when you asked me to visit you? Well, I've got good news...!"

And off I went, crisscrossing the globe like a drunken bull, and, weak from the endless flights and a few too many glasses of champagne, hugging old friends in the airports of Beijing, Casablanca, Rio de Janeiro, Bogotá, Dubai, Buenos Aires, Moscow, Brasilia, Macapá on the edge of the Amazon, Istanbul, São Paulo, Geneva, Seoul, Paris, the Dominican Republic, Athens, Madrid, and Puerto Rico *twice,* once during a hurricane. I even revisited European stalwarts like Paris, Geneva, Athens and Madrid. I've crossed grand rivers and piddly streams, valley rifts and prairies, tundra, mountain ranges and steppes. I've gone from cobblestones to bamboo, Vespas to vipers, glaciers to lava fields, tombs to shipping ports, grilled guinea pig on menus to scorpions on sticks, drunk guaraná açai juice and cocaine tea, seen endless tenement blocks and sparkling palaces. I hope by this stage you are not struggling to force back down the sick that's threatening to shoot up your throat.

With each trip I take, though, my legs cramped, my butt aching, and I peer at the sights through bleary eyes, laugh a bit shrilly with my friends, scrabble for souvenirs, all in a jet-lagged, dreamy, fantasy-like haze. Then I am carted, slightly punch-drunk, back to the airport, and when I touch down at Newark Airport, I stagger off the plane and drag my weary body and muddled head back to work. Usually, it's only weeks or months later that I have the time to sit down, flick through my photos, and be amazed at where I had gone and the great time I had had. I realized I wasn't Jet Set Jerry, I was more Jet Lag Jerry.

Then the trips became more exotic. I branched out to where I knew nobody, asking friends on Facebook if they wanted to come along. Hearty adventurous souls replied. So then it was off to Rome, Machu Picchu, Chichen Itza, Cairo,, even to Kenya on safari! But my three day rule still applied, and even with that, I'm sure, I started to accrue negative vacation days, but I've been able to fulfill my dreams without losing a job or having to file for bankruptcy.

You may wonder if, hazy with jet lag, eyes bloodshot, vision blurry, I visited these places without really discovering them, but I think I managed okay. When you come back from vacation, you're always a bit different; something of the country resides in your heart and in your mind, something new and special that will stay with you always.

It came to me one day that, just by chance, I had managed to see five of the seven Modern Wonders of the World, and also to the lone remaining Ancient Wonder, the Pyramids. They are all amazing places, each trip an amazing story. Why not make them into books? Maybe people will enjoy reading about them. I'll do the Seven Modern Wonders first, I thought, then move further afield. This is the first of the series, and I hope you have as much fun reading it as I had on the trip.

Don't worry, I'll do all the hard work, the standing in line for visas and security, the shriek-inducing vaccinations, the twelve hour flights, the shoving of three days' clothing for two types of weather into the confines of a carry on, the conversion of yuan or reals into dollars and back, the dysentery). You just need to sit back in the comfort of your sofa or bed or subway seat, wherever you happen to be reading this (though in the case of the subway seat, maybe 'comfort' isn't the right word), and travel with me. And, if you're planning a trip yourself, hopefully I'll be able to offer some helpful tips and do's and don'ts.

First stop, Beijing, China, and one of the truly incredible Seven Modern Wonders of the World, the Great Wall. What wonders of the Mysterious Orient did I discover there? What shocks lurk beyond public restroom doors? What flavors of potato chips startle the Western palate? How can you find somebody who speaks English? It's easier than you think. And, once you've hauled yourself up to the lofty Great Wall, how on earth do you get back down? Read and find out!

First, though, a rundown of the new Modern Wonders and their original counterparts, the Seven Ancient Wonders. If you're only interested in Beijing and the Great Wall, please feel free to skip this.

ANCIENT VS. NEW7:

THE SEVEN WONDERS OF THE WORLD

BEIJING AND THE GREAT WALL OF CHINA:

I was a gawky 11-year-old in Mrs. Jasprica's social studies class when I first heard of the Seven Wonders of the World. I think we were studying ancient Greece that week.

My classmates seemed to be struggling to keep their eyes open. These 'wonders' seemed odd and alien, and not terribly interesting. There weren't even any photographs of them, just some illustrations in our tattered textbooks, and they were in black and white! And all the wonders were ancient. When you're eleven, ancient is boring. Call me a nerd, call me a geek, but I was riveted to Mrs. Jasprica's every word (though she herself seemed to be stifling her yawns as she reeled them off for us, preparing herself for a trawl through the list of gods, Hera, Zeus, etc. which was on the next page).

The list was compiled by some guy called Philo of Byzantium in 225 BC.

In case you've forgotten (and I'm sure most of us have), here they are: the Great Pyramid at Giza, the Hanging Gardens of Babylon (*Hmm, I've heard about them from catechism school, don't they have something to do with people speaking in tongues, and maybe they met at these gardens to speak in their tongues,* my 11-year-old self thought), the Statue of Zeus at Olympia (*Zeus is the god of the ancient Greeks, and Olympia is the capital of Washington state,* I thought, as we had done state capitals the month before), the Temple of Artemis at Ephesus, the Mausoleum at Halicarnassus (*where on Earth...?! and what on earth...? Did it have something to do with mice?*), the Colossus of Rhodes, which I only knew must be something very big, and the Lighthouse at Alexandria, which I knew was in Virginia, as we had gone there on vacation the summer before when we went to visit Mount Vernon and George Washington's house, so maybe it was a special lighthouse George Washington had built. But why hadn't we visited it then, if we were so close and it was a wonder of the world?

I raised my hand.

"Mrs. Jasprica?"

"Yes?"

She seemed annoyed at being interrupted. There was so much more she was expected to teach us that day, apparently.

"Could you tell me, we went to Alexandria last summer—"

"We did?!" Her shock was obvious. My classmates stared at me.

"Well, no, I mean, not us, but me and my family."

"I see."

"And, well, if this Lighthouse is such a wonder, why didn't we go visit it?"

As if she had helped plan my dad's itinerary for the trip!

"Are you talking about Egypt?"

"Egypt? No. Virginia."

Thinking back, she must have stifled a hoot of laughter.

"Oh, Gerald, no! Not Alexandria, Virginia. Alexandria, *Egypt*. You couldn't have seen any of these wonders, anyway. Even if you had gone to Egypt. They are *ancient*. They were all destroyed by, hmm, well, fires and earthquakes, it says here. Centuries ago. Well, except for the pyramids. They're still there."

My heart fell. So these wonderful wonders, six of them anyway, didn't even exist anymore. I'd never be able to see them.

Fast forward to 2000, and enter Bernard Weber, a Swiss-Canadian who decided to hold a worldwide popularity contest to discover the 'world's most loved modern wonders. I guess he was tired of the old list of wonders. He rebranded them the New7Wonders of the World, and a foundation with the same name was set up. I guess their first three words were always written together to help with hashtags and such.

Weber gave people around the world seven years to vote from a list of hundreds of amazing spots around the world. Each phone, so therefore each person, was only allowed one text, but as we know, there are ways around that. And you could phone as many times as you wanted. In that sense, it was a bit like the *X Factor* or *American Idol,* where perhaps the best person doesn't win, only the person who got the most votes by whatever means. The Brazilian government, for example, had a massive campaign to ensure as many people as had phones would vote; texts were sent out countrywide, firing the population into a VOTE FOR CHRIST frenzy. Because of campaigns like this, UNESCO and its World Heritage mission, which was set up to encourage conservation of the world's cultural sites, distanced itself from the contest, as it must treat each cultural wonder equally.

The results were finally announced with much fanfare in 2007. Hundreds of millions of people voted, though the exact number, and how many voted for what, and how many might have voted numerous times, is a closely guarded secret, maybe even unknown. Regardless of the controversy, here the New7Wonders are, in the order of when they were built, oldest first: the Great Wall of China (from the 7th Century BC on); Petra, Jordan (c. 100 BC); the Colosseum, Rome, Italy (AD 80); Chichén Itzá, Mexico (c. AD 600); Machu Picchu, Peru (c. AD 1450), the Taj Mahal, Agra, India (c. AD 1648), and the relative infant of the lot, Christ the Redeemer, Rio de Janieio, Brazil, (1931). The Great Pyramid of Giza was given an honorary mention; it couldn't be included because it was already in the list of the Seven Ancient Wonders. It was completed around 2650 BC, so of course it's the oldest on the list.

The runners up included such familiar faces as the Statue of Liberty, the Eiffel Tower and the Acropolis, the perhaps lesser known Stonehenge, Angkor Wat, and Hagia Sophia, and just for a bit of randomness, Timbuktu, Neushwanstein, the Sydney Opera House, Alhamra, the Kremlin and Red Square, the Moai Statues of Chile, and Kiyomizu-Dera in Japan.

At the time, there was a bit of confusion as to why the Statue of Liberty, the Eiffel Tower or Big Ben, say, are not on the list, and why some places fewer people have heard of are. I'm not naming names; I'll leave that to your imagination. Perhaps it is suspect that they seem to be somewhat equally distributed throughout the world, conveniently but perhaps suspiciously multicultural, and with a dearth of old guard, Eurocentric, stalwarts. But, whatever. If the entire world really did vote, perhaps such a result is expected. Regardless of how any of the wonders made the list, they made it, and the list exists and can't be unmade.

What I do find interesting is how many of the wonders are nestled in equally breathtaking scenery. It's like you get two for the price of one; perhaps the surroundings adds to their wonder. For example, with Christ the Redeemer, you get the glory of the Rio harbor; Machu Picchu is nestled high in those wonderful misty mountains; the romance of Rome surrounds the Colosseum. There is that mysterious cavern that leads into Petra. Even the Great Pyramid. If you look one way, it is perched on the polluted and trash-strewn edge of Cairo with a Pizza Hut nearby, but if you turn around, you have the majesty of the Sahara Desert stretching into the horizon.

As I said before, there's a bit of controversy as to how some of the wonders got on that list, and if they deserve it. But I think we can agree that the Great Wall definitely deserves to be on the list. Let's go visit it. But first, we must get to China, or, more apt, the rather more sinister-sounding People's Republic of China. Specifically, Beijing.

BEIJING AND THE GREAT WALL OF CHINA:

BROWN AIR, SLIT PANTS AND TOILETS OF THE DAMNED

GERALD HANSEN

BEIJING AND THE GREAT WALL OF CHINA:

Who knows how (or, indeed, why), but a few years ago, my friends Tina and Taal suddenly upped sticks from New York and found themselves running three restaurants in Beijing. Tina is a successful restaurant manager, Taal an executive chef and wine expert. They had a Mexican restaurant, an American-style cafe, and their flagship store was the Italian Kitchen.

I don't imagine many people put Beijing in the top three of their employment wish list, maybe not even in their top ten. But, as my friends explained, they had been offered a chance of an exciting new life halfway around the world, almost literally, by a friend of Taal's mother. The friend was Chinese. When they asked me to come visit them, I jumped at the chance. "Can we see the Great Wall? Is it near you in Beijing?" I didn't have a clue. I suspected not. It seemed to me the Great Wall was miles from any big city. Tina stifled a laugh. "Of course!" she said. "Nobody goes to Beijing without visiting the Wall."

"What? Really?"

"Yes, it's only two hours away."

Again, maybe you don't view Beijing as a vacation hot spot, but it was the land of my childhood dreams.

As a 14-year-old newly arrived on a military base in Iceland, I'd been struck with a brief, perhaps bizarre, obsession with China. Who knows where it came from. This was back when Beijing was called Peking. I woke up one day, I can't remember exactly when, and the name had suddenly changed. Yet Peking Duck is still Peking Duck. Odd.

I had somehow procured Chinese wall hangings and placed them around my teen bedroom. You know the ones I'm talking about, with a scroll-like thing at either end, a few pagodas in the middle, maybe a Chinese man or woman doing something traditional with fans or swords in the foreground, a few Mandarin characters at the top, and in the background, those romantic jagged mountains stretching off in the distance. Or, rather, up the length of the wall hanging.

My favorite wall hanging, the one I gave pride of place, situated above my desk so I didn't even have to tilt my head or crane my neck to see it, was of the Great Wall. To me it seemed the epicenter of China, the main symbol.

I wanted to master Mandarin. I got a book out of the library, learned five or six characters, wrote them out and, my calligraphy skills lacking, gave up. I was fascinated with pandas and bamboo. I wanted a bonsai tree, but this was Iceland, and I couldn't even find one of those little bamboo plants you can get in any 99 cent store everywhere in the US. The Navy Exchange only had a selection of three shirts for the entire teenage population of the base to wear, so a wide array of plants, let along bonsai trees, was beyond their distribution/shipping capabilities. How I found the wall hangings from the dearth of products on their shelves I can't imagine. With my bedroom window relentlessly rattling because of the wind (it was always windy in Iceland), the empty lava fields stretching out in all directions in the 22-hour winter nights beyond that window, I would sit huddled at my desk, cozy, probably listening to Fleetwood Mac and putting off my homework, and stare up at the cragged mountaintops on the wall hangings, wishing I was in this far off exotic land, not the Iceland I was in fact living in. The irony. (Actually, I'm being disingenuous here, because I was as riveted in Keflavik as a tourist might be in China, and those high school years of mine were a blast; the stories I could tell! The things that went on in those concrete bus shelters around the base while we waited for the bus to take us, well, around the base, and all the shenanigans in the corners of the smoking room of the Youth Center (!). I'm even playing up the scant selection of clothing at the Navy Exchange; there were really about seven shirts to choose from, and a wide array of Icelandic wool sweaters. But after a few months of living anywhere, you begin to take the place for granted and start looking further afield for more excitement.)

On those long Iceland nights, I lived at that desk in a fantasy world. Me getting to China, then getting to the Great Wall, then climbing it, seemed as likely as Stevie Nicks materializing in my bedroom, gypsy shawls aflutter. My 14-year-old self never took into consideration the fact that China was a communist country. It was the ancient China of the Ming or the Qing or the Xia dynasty I was dreaming of. I guess I thought a China pre-1949 People's Revolution still existed, one before the horrific modern changes made by Mao Tse Tung, whose name also mysteriously changed to Mao Zedong one day.

At the time, I was totally totally disregarding a natural wonder of the world, the Aurora Borealis/the Northern Lights, no doubt shimmering through the sky overhead. Had I bothered to open that rattling window, but it was too cold to do that. Many people were no doubt wishing they were where I was at that very moment. The entire family did gather outside the house the first winter and stare up at it through the chilly air with wonder once, maybe twice, but after that, it was just there.

My China obsession petered out after a few months, as teenage obsessions tend to. It was replaced by, of all things, archaeology, but now I had a chance to visit China for myself.

Did the remnants of the China of my dreams still exist in some form? Or had everything been replaced by a very different China? It was my chance to find out.

In New York, I dragged myself out of bed at some ungodly hour in the morning and staggered to the Chinese consulate. It was inconveniently located miles from any subway station. The lines were long. As I waited the three days for my visa to be approved—not in the consulate itself; we were allowed to leave and then come back to pick it up—I started dropping into conversations as casually as I could, "I'm just waiting for my visa to be approved for China. I'm going to visit Tina and Taal. And to see the Great Wall."

Jaws dropped. Friends took a step back.

"Communist China?"

"You mean that repressive country with no regard for basic human rights?"

"Tourists are attacked in dark alleys and wake up missing their kidneys and livers and other organs. And their stomachs aren't even properly stitched up! It'll happen to you, too!"

(With a vehement shake of the head) "They hate Americans so much there, the government took down the Starbucks at the entrance of the Great Wall after the indigenous people revolted against it."

"You are making me uncomfortable with talk of this trip. Please move away from me."

And, again, "Kidneys and livers are in great demand over there! You'll never get out alive."

So that was that decided, then. It would be my first exciting trip to an exotic location, and my last. I would be butchered at the hands of organ traffickers.

And one last remark: "Don't you know about the Tianamen Square massacre?"

This gave me pause for thought. As a Cold War child, that

Iron Curtain dividing the communist world from the 'free' one was still in my mind, though the Berlin Wall had fallen decades before. Most people my age regarded communist countries with pity and fear, had visions of barbed wire and machine gun-toting secret police, concrete blocks of buildings with no phones and endless lines for loaves of stale bread. My friends seemed similarly afflicted.

The reality of where I was going sunk into my brain, but it didn't make me any less excited to go pick up my visa. I had paid enough for it, after all ($160, I believe). Though now I was excited and fearful in equal measures.

China has a bad reputation, and with good reason. Although, I don't know about you, but lately it seems to me Chinese tourists have started appearing everywhere in New York, as if they were citizens of a regular country, not a communist regime. How they suddenly got visas, I can't imagine. And I keep overhearing people on the subway saying things like, "When I went to Shanghai..." and "They lost our luggage in Macau..." so something must have changed to make it a tourist destination for Americans as well.

Before this shift, though, I got my visa, and kept flipping open my passport to the page and inspecting it, and all the while I couldn't shake from my mind that I wouldn't be entering any country, I would be entering COMMUNIST CHINA. The land of government crackdowns and purges. The land of the Great Leap Forward (which ended up being ten steps back) of 1958-62; it was a nationwide government-enforced plan to change China from a farming country to a city country. It led to the Great Famine and tens of millions of deaths by starvation (anywhere from 18 to 55 million). It was the land of the Cultural Revolution (1966-1976), causing what seems to be the usual suspects of any repressive regime, the persecutions of millions, the torture, the public humiliations, the seizing of property, the arbitrary imprisonments, the enforced hard labor, the youths of the Red Guard banging on your door in the middle of the night, forcing you and your extended family out of the city and into the farmland to harvest wheat as part of the government's Down To The Countryside Movement. This seems to me the opposite of the Great Leap Forward, so did the government uproot whole families from the countryside, then force them back a few years later? Please pardon my ignorance, and if you can shed some light on this, please do tell me. At the helm of all this violence and misery in the name of the good of the party was the newly-spelled Mao Tzedong, who I would soon see on coffee mugs and key chains in every souvenir stall of Beijing. Yes, a man with the blood of millions on his communist style coat and buttons fondly remembered by the nation as a whole today as a kindly grandfatherly George Washington-type figure. Go figure.

And if all this seems like history as ancient as the original seven wonders to you, then there was the aforementioned relatively recent Tianamen Square Massacre of 1989, called the June Fourth 'Incident' by the Chinese government still, where students protesters were set upon by flanks of assault weapons and tanks. Though the death toll this time around was a relatively modest 'hundreds to thousands,' not tens of millions, this doesn't account for the crackdown that followed, and the purges of the sympathetic.

This was where I was going to spend my vacation.

I threw some clothes into a bag, checked the exchange rate of yuan to dollar, and did a few fantasy transactions to be sure I wasn't ripped off when buying souvenirs. Figured out how much a meal at McDonalds should cost, so I could compare it to the price when I got there. It was impossible to finally learn Chinese (and should it be Mandarin or Cantonese?) in a few days, so, armed only with "ni hao' (hello) and 'shey shey" (thank you), I boarded the plane for the 14-hour journey.

With both Chinas vying for attention in my brain, and feeling like a traitor to my country, I approached the customs podium/pulpit. Maybe it was my imagination, but it seemed they were very high, as if they wanted to inspect us capitalists from on high, to assert their superiority The uniforms appeared to me more repressive and sinister than they ought to. As an aside, I took a second trip to visit Tina and Taal, I didn't notice any of this at all. The customs podiums at the Beijing Airport are the same height as any other podium around the world. It must have been my fear of the unknown.. Or maybe the podiums had been lowered in the interim.

Tina and I screamed with delight and hugged each other, jumping up and down at the baggage carousel. Tina is tall and has a marvelous laugh that can turn heads at any party. She's full of fun, a bit wild, and a food connoisseur, an adventurer. Taal stood by and looked wryly on. He's more laid back, soft-spoken and measured. They are a great match. Yin and Yang, which is quite apt considering where we were. At times, Taal seemed to whisper. I didn't know if he was speaking so low because he always did, or if he didn't want to draw attention to himself with his English. But, checking out the throngs milling around us waiting for their luggage to materialize on the conveyor belt, I think a glance at the three of us would suffice to let everyone else know Chinese wasn't our native language.
  "Ohhh, it's so great to be speaking to an American!" Tina

bubbled. "You have no idea how hard it's been for us lately. They've blocked Facebook and YouTube, sometimes they block CNN... We've been going crazy!"

They were starved for English speaking partners. So ex-pats in China were even cut off from the home comforts of the internet! Perhaps this really was a totalitarian regime after all. CNN broadcasting was spotty, Taal explained, the government suddenly cut off reports in the middle seemingly at random. Maybe they suspect something on the news channel was offensive, or something being reported might lead to a revolt.

"Our driver is waiting outside," Tina said, a bit embarrassed. "His name's Cheng."

I raised an eyebrow. I started to understand why they had moved to China. It was like when we lived in Thailand. Suddenly we had a maid and a cook and a gardener. No doubt they did too, with the exception of the gardener, as I knew they lived in a high-rise. Maybe someone was in their apartment polishing the silver even as we spoke.

We got my luggage.

I saw it the moment we stepped out of the airport. Air you could chew. At first I thought there was a problem with my sight, a side effect of jet lag. Or that I was hallucinating. My eyes seemed to be flooded with 'floaters.' It was as if I could actually see the particles of air. And those particles were brown.

"The...air...!" I gasped into the fug.

Tina and Taal smiled. Taal said, "When it gets really bad—"

"Isn't this really bad?"

They hooted with laughter.

"Welcome to Beijing!" they chimed.

The air in Beijing needs to be seen to be believed, 'seen'

being the operative word. There is a constant eruption of smoke from a multitude of Industrial-Revolution-type factory chimneys that crowd the city, without any regard for the environment. Instinctively you want to gag, you feel like it's an effort to take in lungsful of this fetid air, a trial to expel it from your lungs as quickly as you can without infecting them. But after a few breaths in and out, it seems you can indeed breathe normally. You get used to it. Or, I did, anyway.

"So, as I was saying," Taal continued as the car drove towards the city, "when the air gets really bad, and there are towers that monitor that, there's you can see one right outside the window of our living room, actually, they send up rockets to sort of shake the air, and form rain clouds, so that it rains and cleans the air. So they we get what they call a 'Blue Sky Day,' or a 'Big/Good Day,' properly translated."

This sounded very sci-fi and a little creepy, and who this mysterious 'they' might be was on the verge of giving me sleepless nights during my stay there, but, as I later learned—for we did have a Blue Sky Day—whatever 'they' do *does* clear the air, and you can notice the difference the moment you walk outside the next morning. (I've since discovered that maybe it isn't secret communist artificial rain making rockets, and only the fact that the government forces the factories to stop for a few days.) But as the Blue Sky Day goes on, the pollution accumulates, and the air you are breathing gets dirtier and dirtier, thicker and thicker, and more and more brown. People with hospital face masks, like Michael Jackson used to wear, start appearing on the streets. It's a very common sight. Maybe they are just a few decades behind as far as the environment is concerned. Apparently, Pittsburgh was just as bad not too long ago, and wasn't Los Angeles once renowned for being hidden under permanent smog?

Tina leaned forward and, to my amazement, spoke to Cheng the driver...in Chinese!

Had she suddenly done the splits there on the floor of the car, I would've been less surprised.

"Tina! Wow!"

"It's so hard to learn. I had a private tutor when we first got here. I can get by, but I'm not great."

But...yes, she was! I remembered my foolish attempts at the language as a child in my bedroom, my five or six words. I'd always rated her, but now she was my new hero!

As people do, I stared eagerly out the windows as we spoke, hungry to see the new country I had landed in. But it seemed the same as any airport drive into an exciting city, boring except for signs in a different language. Nothing but guard rails and some grass and trees. Cars and highway guard rails look the same all over the world. Admittedly, there are some countries where that drive is slightly different, for example, there might be palm trees or firs or some other type of tree different to the ones you have at home, or the wall of a warehouse covered in graffiti in a different language, and those cause a ripple of excitement, but usually it's the least exciting part of any trip.

"We've got great restaurants lined up for you to eat in. No, not our own, but you'll be having breakfast from the cafe today, then lunch at the Mexican Kitchen and the Italian Kitchen. I;m excited for you to try them out. But you're in China, so of course you've got to eat Chinese food. And there are so many types. And they are all delicious." I knew Tina was a foodie, so I trusted her judgment. "Tonight, we'll go to a restaurant that has the spiciest food I've found in Beijing. It's Szechuan, and it's called the Five Men's Heads. I know you love spicy food. Tomorrow, we'll have Shanghai food, Hu cuisine, I think it's called, and they have desserts of shaved ice. And then, the best place near us which has Peking Duck. You know you can't leave Beijing without having Peking Duck!"

"I've always wondered, why isn't it called Peking Duck?"

"I don't know, but even here, it's called Peking Duck."

Stranger and stranger.

"You know we won't be able to show you around today, we have to work, but I'll take one day off to show you the Wall." Tina squeezed my hand eagerly. "I know you've always wanted to see it."

We jabbered on excitedly, filling each other in on what had happened since we last met.

"I wish," Tina said, and there was a wistful sigh, "I had been here to see the Beijing of a million bike bells ringing out on the streets. Though...maybe the ringing of a million bike bells outside my window at 8 o'clock in the morning would've driven me—sorry, I've got to take this call. It's one of the restaurants. We're catering a big party tonight at one of the ex-pat's mansions."

As Tina rattled off things in Chinese down the line, then screamed a bit, then laughed, then rattled off more Chinese, Taal explained their situation. The American cafe they ran was across the street from their apartment high rise, but the other two were located on a compound inside an ex-pat gated community. I had wondered how many Chinese would be interested in Mexican or Italian cuisine, and it seemed not many. The restaurants were there mainly to appeal to non-Chinese businessmen and -women and their families. There was also a nearby street outside the compound, in 'real' Beijing, which was filled with bars and nightclubs that catered to tourists, American or otherwise. There seemed to be very few Americans living there, Taal said, so when he and Tina finally had the chance to speak English to somebody besides each other, the English speakers were all from non-English speaking countries, most of them Europe, none of them fluent. Their skill ranged from beginner to low advanced. Nobody spoke fluently. All seemed to speak an English devoid of any accent. It wasn't American, it wasn't British, not Australian or New Zealand, not Irish or Scottish or Welsh. An eerie, bland Globish English, stripped of all character. Finally, they had me to speak to. I'd use as much slang as I could to make them happy.

With Tina still babbling down the line, Taal said to me, "Let me share a few things with you about Beijing, so you're not surprised when you see them. I don't want to scare you..."

But he did, a bit.

The first thing was the restrooms. Citywide, they were still in transition from the traditional squat-style to the modern Western version of a toilet bowl. (I've since learned that China is not alone in this respect, and countries as diverse as Turkey and Greece also had the squat toilets until recently. But back then, I was clueless as to what a squat toilet might be.)

"A...a what?" I wondered?

Taal explained that everywhere you went, if you had the urge or necessity to relieve yourself, you never knew as you were approaching the restroom what you might find inside: ancient, traditional, modern, or, most common, a mixture. Even in pricey restaurants where you might feel safe, he explained, there was still the luck of the draw.

If you're out of luck, you will be confronted by a toilet of the damned, a trough toilet. It's as horrible (or as thrilling) as the name suggests. You walk in, and it is just a room, usually dingy and maybe with peeling paint on the walls. Not a stall to be seen. Only a long metal trough. Maybe that's fine if you're a man and you only need to urinate. Indeed, I've even seen a similar set up in some bars in New York. But if are a woman or if your needs are more substantial, you must tug down your trousers/hike up your dress or skirt, squat down (next to a stranger, if you're unlucky enough to find yourself in a busy bathroom), and, with the few trickles of water that are the 'flushing' system creeping down the wall behind your back, do your business.

If you're a bit luckier, the second type has, to your relief (somewhat), squat toilets. These are at least designed for an individual toilet experience. If you're even luckier, there will be doors on the stalls for a private individual toilet experience. Beyond the doors (or not), there is a lone hole in the floor and indentations for your feet, and, without the aid of handles on the wall, you are expected to balance yourself, squat and hover your butt over what you half-hope isn't and half-fear is a bottomless pit. You must aim carefully.

Next up are the toilets with stalls equipped with the luxury of a door, though it's a surprise what may or may not lurk behind those doors. If there is a line for the bathroom, you must take the first stall that becomes available, and you'll be either dismayed or delighted at what you find. Delighted if you spy a toilet bowl, no matter how stained, dismayed if it's a squat toilet. Some places have both traditional and modern toilets, and there are little signs indicating which is which, and, if so, you can always motion for someone in the line to go ahead of you if it's a squat toilet that becomes available first. Or, if you're adventurous, you can wait for the squat toilet, when in Rome and all that.

In the upcoming days, I would slowly realize I wasn't brave enough to try a squat toilet, and fortune did indeed smile down upon me, as I used only Western toilet bowls. I spent each visit to a restroom trying to repress what horrors lurked beyond the second type of door. Though I did peer into a few other toilets with disbelief and disgust, but also, I must admit, with a special little thrill. It's something you don't see every day in New York City, though there are other things (homeless men taking a shit on the subway platform, for example) that vie for strangeness. Maybe, out of curiosity, morbid or not, you are wondering what they look like, and are cursing the lack of photo. But when I was there, I had no idea I'd be writing this book, and they are something you hope to never see again, let alone capture forever in a photo for sentimental memories.

It came to me one day, though, that I had been thinking of the trough toilets and squat ones as the bathrooms not having been properly renovated yet, and that was the wrong way to think. Maybe the existence of traditional toilets in modern Beijing isn't a matter of lack of renovation. Maybe it's because that isn't what some people want. Who are we in the West to impose Western toilet habits upon others? Some people must prefer to squat, and it's supposed to be healthier. Some older Chinese might even stare in incomprehension when they enter a toilet bowl stall, wondering how to perch themselves atop one. That might explain why most bathrooms are a mixture of both. So that people can do their business however they want. Either that, or it was cheaper for the management of the restaurant to leave the squat toilets in.

Should I have brought my own toilet paper? I wondered, suddenly fearful. Taal told me it isn't necessary. Although the toilet paper varied in texture from sandpaper to tracing paper depending on the venue, the restrooms were always well stocked.

He then went on to tell me about slit pants. To my shock. Apparently, children from infants until the age of two or three, boys and girls alike, wear them. They are shorts with a slit in the rear, so that busy mothers don't need to waste time with diapers and the finding of public restrooms. When the child (I was going to say children, but each parent until very recently could only have one, according to government regulations) needs to go potty, their slit pants allow them to squat wherever they happen to be, no bushes or hidden alleyways needed, and let it go. I'm guessing they don't wear any underwear; it would defeat the purpose of the slit pants. Leaving alone for the moment what state the fabric on the edges of the slits might be in, I wondered who was responsible for pick up duty. Was the busy mother expected, like an American dog owner, to pull out a plastic bag and pick it up and search for the closest trash receptacle? Or, I wondered later, having seen so many men in uniforms around the streets of Beijing doing clean up, was there a man in a uniform whose government-mandated job it was to clean the mess up?

I've since learned that, in modern Beijing, slit pants are supposedly in decline, becoming somewhat of an endangered species. If you ask the Chinese, they'll say they are mainly worn nowadays in the villages, not the modern cities. But then you ask those born in Beijing if they wore them as children (and I've asked plenty), and they chorus, "Of course!" But maybe this is true because they are older. Perhaps the new generation has moved on to the modern convenience of diapers.

Tina finally hung up. There were a lot of problems with that catering job, apparently. The anonymous scenery beyond the guard rails was becoming perking up as fields and trees were giving way to small streets and houses, Chinese characters on every store window, a pagoda or two, then larger streets and bigger buildings...

Tina said something to Cheng, and he replied. I had the feeling we would soon be home.

BEIJING AND THE GREAT WALL OF CHINA:

WELCOME TO BEIJING

BEIJING AND THE GREAT WALL OF CHINA:

The moment I stepped inside Tina and Taal's Beijing apartment, I understood one of the reasons they might have left New York for China. As a New Yorker like them, I'm used to bathrooms where you can lean over and turn on the shower while wiping your butt, closets that are tiny slits in the wall. Not only did they have house staff, they had space. Compared to usual New York apartment sizes, Tina and Taal's Beijing apartment was palatial. The moment Chan, the housekeeper (!), opened the door, I saw parquet flooring stretching as far as the eye could see. Floor to ceiling windows. Looking out on a vast expanse of brown air and the chrome, concrete and glass of modern high rises typical of any large city, but also on strangely-shaped skyscrapers and neon signs in Chinese.

"Gerald, we need to take off our shoes here," Tina warned,

handing me a pair of slippers. "Not because we've suddenly turned Chinese, though it is an Asian custom, but because God only knows what's on those sidewalks out there."

With the slit pants, what indeed. She went on to explain that spitting was as common as breathing on the sidewalks of Beijing.

"Who knows what they are all spitting out," Taal said.

Maybe chunks of brown air that had gotten lodged in their lungs.

"First things first," Tina said. "You must be starving. I know I am. Let's put our orders in for breakfast."

I looked around, expecting a cook in an apron and white hat to materialize, but, though the housekeeper sometimes cooked for them, she only knew Chinese dishes, and Tina wanted to break me into Chinese cuisine slowly. She handed me a menu (proudly, as she and Taal had designed it). It was from their American cafe across the street. Customers who wanted to eat there had to enter through a gym (!), and walk to the back, past the changing rooms, to get to the restaurant door. Tina assured me, with strange Chinese planning permission rules—apparently anything goes—this was not at all an odd set up.

I ordered Eggs Benedict, feeling a bit guilty. But there would be plenty of time for Chinese food later. Tina had made all those restaurant reservations.

While we waited for our food to arrive, Tina and Taal had a brief discussion as to whether to register me with the government as a guest. Apparently, they were under some obligation to register all guests, no matter how long they were staying (in my case, three days). Here I felt the specter of a repressive regime pressing down on those who happen to live within its borders. Tina decided not to bother, so that was that. (My next visit, however, Taal decided to register me. He would sleep easier at night, he said. We had to travel to some bizarre office in the middle of nowhere with endless corridors filled with people who looked like they had been there for days sitting on plastic chairs. I was clueless as to what was going on, as everything was in Chinese, but finally I was handed a piece of paper, in Chinese, of course, which I had to keep in my passport until I left. I think Tina slept less well about my registration, and I can understand; she must have felt more repressed.)

"It's too bad we can't go out sightseeing with you today," Tina said as we ate. "But we've got to work."

I understood, and I realized that the palatial apartment and the luxury of a colonial-like house staff came at a price. Working at times 16-hour days and dealing with staff in a foreign language, and dealing with a different culture. It's difficult enough to run a restaurant, what with staffing problems and delivery problems (and for Tina and Taal, where to find things alien in China like tortillas and taco shells and spaghetti and tiramisu), cooking problems and customer satisfaction problems. And as if running one restaurant wasn't enough, they were running three! And in two different locations. All the common stresses were compounded when dealing with another mind set, knowing that all the heads around you are thinking in a different language. The Chinese, apparently, pay high regard in particular to 'saving face,' and some other Chinese thought processes seem incomprehensible to Westerners; there are imagined slights and strange oneupmanships. I had had to deal with a different culture when I lived in Berlin, where every head around me was thinking in German (well, even my own, after a while). And there were times when my English-speaking self regretted being there, especially during a long cold night, and Berlin has a seemingly endless winter, so there were plenty of them.

As we ate breakfast, several maps of Beijing were unfolded before my cup of coffee, a subway map, a street map, and a map showing the location and little drawings of the biggest tourist sites. Tour guides appeared from I don't know where.

"Have a look through these," Tina said. "And choose where you want to go."

"Most people," Taal said, "want to see the Forbidden City."

"And Tianamen Square."

"They're right beside each other, so that's easy."

"And then you might want to go to one of the temples. Maybe the Temple of Heaven. That's the most popular."

"And do you want to go shopping in the markets?"

"You can get every brand there."

"Cheap."

"Probably fake, but cheap."

"They look real enough, though."

"And there are plenty of lesser-known sights to see too."

"Maybe you should take a tour of the hutongs."

"Hmm," Tina mused. "I haven't done that myself. I'd love to do it."

"What are the hutongs?" I asked.

"The old neighborhoods of the city."

"Years ago, the government razed whole sections of the city to build modern buildings, skyscrapers."

"They probably displaced millions of people."

"But some parts were lucky and still stand."

"And the people live there like twenty, fifty, maybe hundreds of years ago. Hmm, I don't know. Do they have electricity, Taal?"

"Some do," he replied.

I gripped Tina's arm with excitement and stabbed at a page

in a tour guide before me.

"Oh, my God! This looks fantastic!"

"What is it?"

"The Underground City!"

Tina and Taal looked at me, blank.

"The what?"

"The Underground City! It says here...uh, it was a complex built when the Chinese were scared of being bombed by the Soviet Union. Wow! It's like, like, a bomb shelter as big as a city! With, would you believe it? Restaurants, schools, movie theaters, factories, even a roller skating rink! More than 33 square miles! Twenty-five feet under the ground! 'Damp, dark, genuinely eerie,' it says here, and admission is only 10 yuan!"

Now they were a bit worried, a bit skeptical.

"Are you sure...?"

They pressed pages of pagodas and dragons into my hand more tightly, changing the position of the photos under the light to make the traditional sites that bit more alluring.

"Wouldn't you rather...?"

I looked down. The Temple of Heaven, the imperial sacrificial altar. Delightful.

"No, I wouldn't."

Now they were giving me looks that said, "It's your grave."

"I'll do all of that today. Tianamen Square, the Forbidden City, maybe I'll make it to the hutongs, but I'm really excited about the Underground City! You guys don't have a phrase book, do you? In case I need to say something?"

"Sorry, no," Tina said. "I've got my Chinese textbooks, but you can't lug one of those around."

"Maybe I should write down a few things."

They called someone, maybe it was the butler, and he wrote down some simple phrases for me on a piece of paper there at the breakfast table. That piece of paper got increasingly tattered as the three days went on. It contained things like how much, where is, hello, goodbye and thank you, with not only the pronunciation in English letters, but also the Chinese characters, because I knew if you got the sounds right (which was iffy) but the inflection wrong (which was probable), they would stare at you in incomprehension. It's difficult to speak Chinese, so you must 'show' Chinese.

Tina's phone rang, then Taal's, then they glanced at the clock. They grimaced.

"We'd better get to work," Taal said.

"Sorry about deserting you like this," Tina said.

But it was no problem at all. I understood they had to work.

She reached into her pocket. "We've never used the subway." They had Cheng. "But I know you need some coins to get the tickets. They won't take bills. They'll scream at you if you try to give them one, apparently."

This didn't deter me, especially when I found out a subway ride cost 2 yuan. Thirty cents. Giving me a map and pointing me in the direction of a subway station in a foreign city and telling me to be on my way fills me with excitement, not dread. I said as much.

Tina looked relieved as she slipped into her jacket.

"I'll be fine," I said. "As long as the subway maps and signs are also in English."

"After the Olympics, they are."

The 2008 Olympics, it seemed, changed everything. The formerly closed country realized it would soon be the showcase for millions of tourists from all over the world, and there had been a massive campaign to make everything more accessible in English. Thank God I hadn't visited in 2007. It must have been a nightmare. Though...did the government even allow tourists back then?

BEIJING AND THE GREAT WALL OF CHINA:

I was equal measures relieved and sad I hadn't made it to Beijing pre-Olympics, before the changes for Westerners had all been made. The land of 10 million chiming bike bells during the morning rush hour, and no McDonalds, no Starbucks, only tepid water to drink and insects on a stick to eat.

"Oh, and just to be on the safe side, make sure you go to the bathroom before you go," Taal warned.

They went off to manage and cook at the compound. A short shower and, yes, comfort break later, I was propelled, unarmed and unprepared except for my piece of paper, out of the American apartment and into the Chinese of the surrounding city and the teeming masses that lived there.

BEIJING AND THE GREAT WALL OF CHINA:

THE SUBWAY

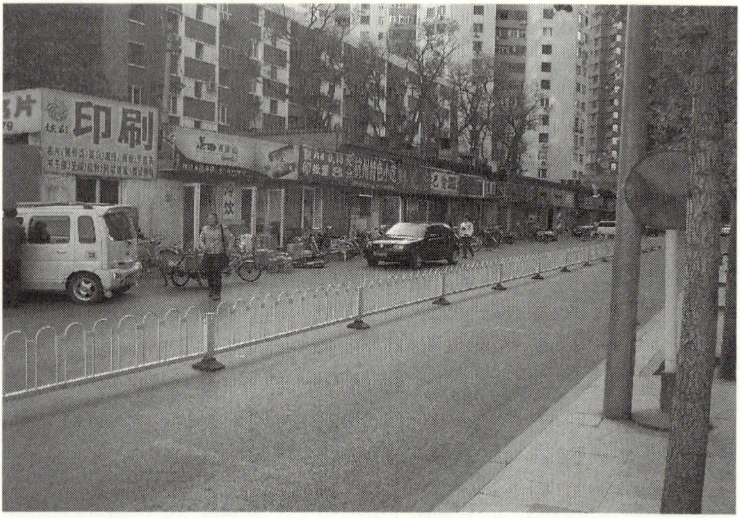
印刷

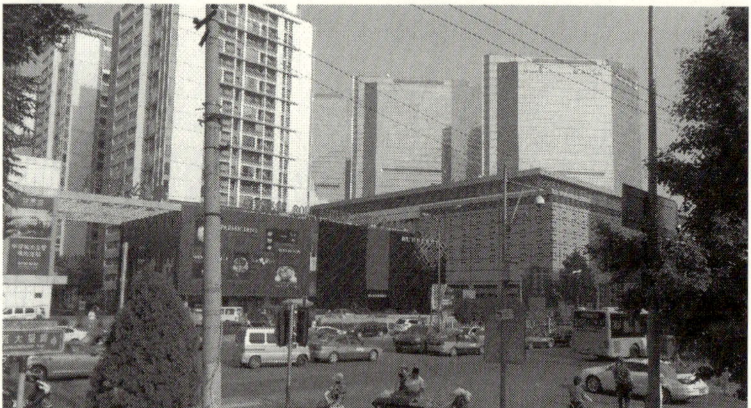

BEIJING AND THE GREAT WALL OF CHINA:

People have asked me the main difference between New York and Beijing and, although it might seem banal and a bit obvious, it was quite important to me: it seems everyone in Beijing is Chinese. I noticed it the moment I stepped outside. Even in the cities of other Asian countries, multicultural thrives. You can see blacks, Hispanics, and whites. It's different in China. If you are not of Chinese descent, you are the lone foreigner, the only one not spitting. Even at the tourist spots.

I stepped outside and peered through the brown air, my bloodshot eyes weary but not wary. Eager. The subway stop was only a few blocks away. There were mechanical cats with one waving paw in practically every shop window, for good luck. One side of each street was traditional, undeveloped, reeking of crime, dirt, poverty, and conjuring up images of opium dens and old Fu Manchu movies. I loved it! How exciting! While on the other side, a different kind of excitement was on offer: retail therapy and conspicuous consumption. Gleaming Burberry, Chanel and Louis Vuitton mega stores that dwarfed Macy's in size flanked the streets. They were heavily guarded.

I say 'street,' but when the government modernized the city, the lowly street seemed not to have interested developers. It seems they only built boulevards. Eight lane boulevards.

Some bikes were still there on the packed boulevards, along with donkey carts piled high with cages of chickens and carts of pigs. There were pushcarts, pedicabs and a dilapidated rickshaw or two, vying for space on the streets packed with shining BMWs and Rolls Royces, oil tankers, accordion buses and massive trucks adding to the brown air. But the rickshaws and the donkey carts were the China of the past, not this new modern China thrusting into the future with

wealth and might clutched firmly in its hands, and all the confidence bordering on arrogance that goes along with this. The sleeping giant bulldozing itself onto the world stage with a swagger. Hawking and
spitting its way into the future. It was nice to see that, even on these
modern boulevards, a bit of an ancient China we Westerners, or I, at least, hanker for still exists.

Among all the men dressed in Armani suits and women in Chanel pencils skirts and Louboutin high heels rushing past, I saw, believe it or not, a few of those rice-farmer conical hats, and even those light blue Mao jackets with the collar that fits close to the neck and the patch pockets, and plenty of 'worker's' caps. That's Beijing, the modern juxtaposed with the traditional almost everywhere you look. And I saw many varieties of uniforms, from the sidewalk sweeping uniform to the leaf raking uniform, to the lamp post cleaning uniform. It was communist China, after all, so there had to be a job for everyone, even if it was raking leaves.

The subway entrance mirrored everything I would find inside: sleek and modern. There was a security check to go through first, with all bags riffled through by, of course, uniformed guards. Large containers of liquid, I saw, were being confiscated, so each subway station is treated, in effect, like a mini-airport. At least I didn't have to take off my shoes. There were refreshingly few ads, though the walls were covered with many 'propaganda' posters, mainly showcasing the power of Chinese athletes and the smiles of attractive young Chinese women.

I needed to get a ticket. There were machines, and although there was an English option, I wanted to interact with people other than Tina and Taal. I approached the ticket counter. It is here that I learned the Chinese seem to have no concept of lining up for things. Grandmothers, teenagers, businessmen shoved me aside and marched to the window. At first I thought it had to do with my slightly-less-than-human status, and I was a bit upset, but then I looked around and realized everybody was doing it to everybody else. Lines are not lines in China, they are a free-for-all, and only the fittest survive, or in this case, get to the cashier.

The subways are like London, where you wave the ticket at an electronic gate, a laser reads it, and the gate whirrs open. You must remember to keep your ticket to slip it into the exit or the gate won't open. I shudder to think what might happen if you lose your ticket and have to appeal to someone in a uniform to get you out. The station wasn't crowded, as trains come every three minutes during rush hour, seven minutes other times. Dirt cheap and efficient. Top marks all around.

Though I dearly love the NYC subway, it gets more expensive every year, and there are fewer trains. Anyone who has had the misfortune to wait forty minutes to board a train at 2 AM and find it packed like it was rush hour knows what I'm talking about. Thank you, MTA, for finally giving us signs that indicate when the next train is coming, but you were about ten years behind the times compared to Beijing (and the subways of any other large city worldwide, I suspect). And why is it so difficult to find a subway map? Do you not know tourists visit us in droves? Even I need a subway map at times, but there are never any to be found.

No problem with maps in the Beijing subway. They are displayed everywhere and, for this trip, there was a little icon of Forbidden City, which is off Tianamen Square, smack dab in the middle of the subway line, and the city itself. So it was easy to find out what train I had to take. Thanks to the Olympics.

Between the stations, through the train windows you see, instead of the black of the tunnel walls and the pipes and whatnot, with an occasional flash of graffiti from the 80s (like in NY), LED light shows in bright colors of happy scenes, children and puppies and rainbows whizzing by. Red lights on the subway line sign that runs the length of the train near the ceiling show you the stops you've traveled, green lights show the stops the train has yet to go. Stops were announced, somewhat unexpectedly and much appreciated, in English after the Chinese. They were spoken in a 1950's British librarian grandmother over-pronounced Received Pronunciation English. I think she even said, "Mind The Gap," even though there wasn't one.

Next to Tianamen Square and the Forbidden City is the Military Museum of the Chinese People's Revolution, which

I had seen in one of the tour guides earlier. A tourist trifecta! I may as well fit that in too. Why not? Know your enemy, and all that.

BEIJING AND THE GREAT WALL OF CHINA:

TIANAMEN SQUARE

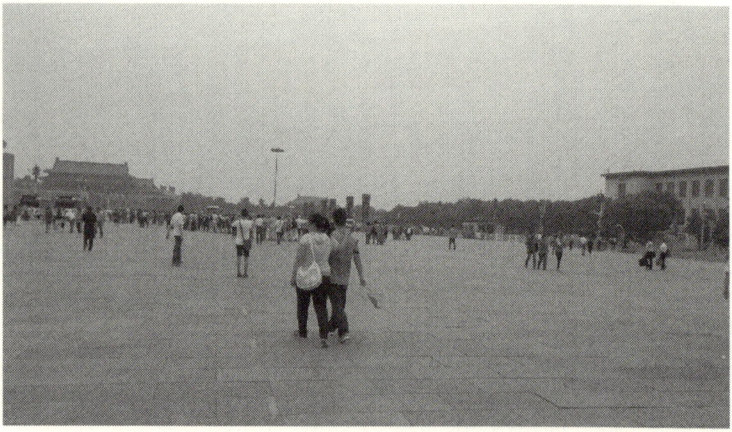

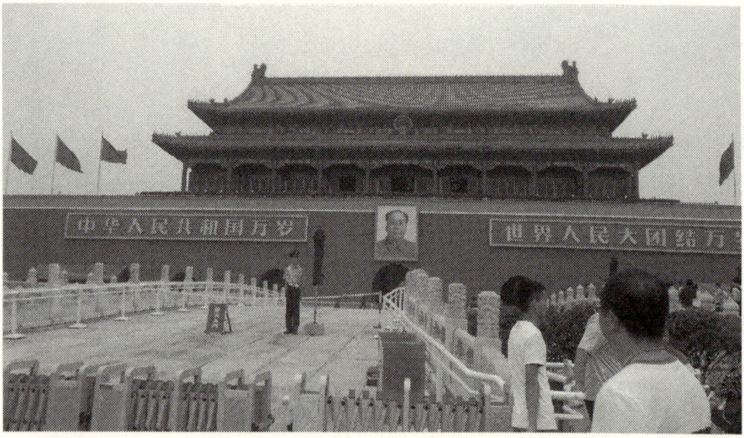
中华人民共和国万岁
世界人民大团结万

BEIJING AND THE GREAT WALL OF CHINA:

Tianamen Square is massive. It seems to stretch off in the distance for miles. Except for the Monument to the People's Heroes in the middle, and Mao's Mausoleum, the National Museum of China and the Great Hall of the People which flank the sides, there's not much there. Except paving and bad memories.

It's where the students flocked to cheer and wave flags at the formation of the People's Republic in 1949, and where, generations later, students gathered to protest the totalitarian regime, only to be shot down. They had tried to revolt, just like all the other communist countries around then had done and succeeded. It was 1989, after all, and overthrowing totalitarian regimes was the done thing that year. But the Chinese military was mightier than the Eastern European countries' armies, I suppose. Maybe from sheer might of numbers. There are almost 1.4 billion people in China, and the military has more than 2 million troops, the largest in the world. All the student earnestness in the world couldn't dissuade them.

I snapped a few photos. I was cursing myself for not having a Smart phone with a selfie mode. The only way I could get myself in a photo would be by asking a passing Chinese person to take one for me. This could easily be done with gestures, and the people around me seemed friendly enough; they didn't appear as if they'd race off with my camera. Also, one of the phrases on my piece of paper was "Hello. Would you please take a photo of me?" But I didn't trust myself to ask anybody. Photos of Tianamen Square without me would have to do. But I was determined to pull that paper out when I got to the Forbidden City, and definitely when I got to the Underground City. I hurried across eight lanes of slinky buses, rickshaws, taxis and trucks to get the Forbidden City. Chairman Mao's smiling face welcomed me from a massive frame hung on the entrance. Chinese flags fluttered in the breeze from the roof. It was scary and impressive at the same time.

BEIJING AND THE GREAT WALL OF CHINA:

THE FORBIDDEN CITY

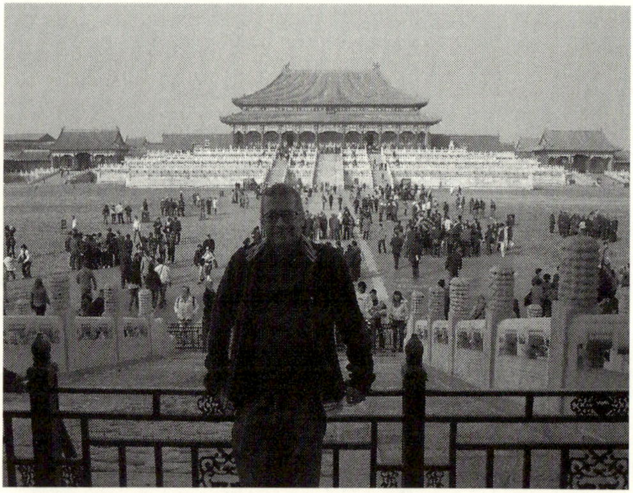

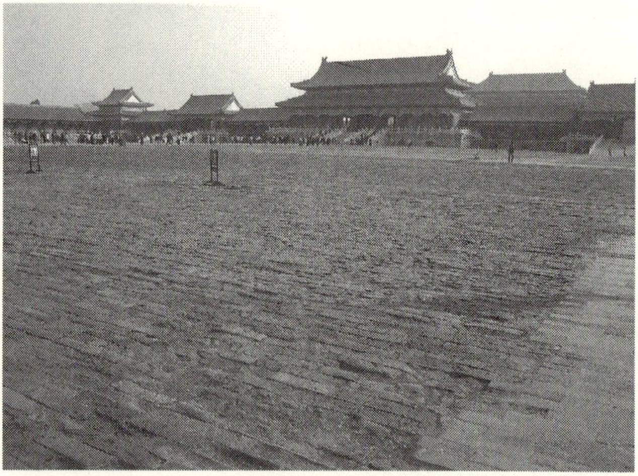

But not quite as scary as the 'line' to buy tickets. After the subway, though, I knew what to do: shove and elbow my way to the front. It seemed to me you can push and tug people as much as you want, and nobody will be offended. It's as if you hadn't touched them, hadn't invaded their 'person space.' It's the Chinese way, and it's refreshing. It's a far cry from the people, elsewhere, who snap, with glinting eyes that threaten a frivolous lawsuit they might just win "Don't touch me!"

As I shoved my way into the screaming, heaving throngs corralling the ticket counter window and the harried, barking women behind the glass, I felt a tap on my shoulder. I whipped around, shocked. Was it the cops? Were foreigners not allowed to shove like the Chinese? My pounding heart stilled as I looked at a kindly non-Chinese face. The only other one in the 'line.' A South American guy, if I wasn't mistaken.

"Excuse me," he said. "But I notice you look like you know what you're doing. And we seem to be the only non-Chinese tourists here. I wonder...would you like to accompany me around the Forbidden City? We could take photos of each other."

As if my prayers had been heard. A good friend of mine says I can manifest things. Maybe it's true.

We got our tickets, which were 60 yuan, about $9. In other words, pennies, compared to other sights I've been to around the world. As we crossed the moat (yes, there it one!) and passed the military guards that lined the entrance to made our way inside, we introduced ourselves. His name was Fercho, and he was a university professor from Bogotá, Colombia. He spoke, and at length, about exactly how each shot should be

framed, and as each requirement was laid out, the more fixed my smile became, the heavier my heart. But he ended up being a great companion at the Forbidden City, and he was an expert photographer. I'd only been gone from Tina and Taal's apartment for an hour or so, but already I was grateful to have someone to speak English with. And to take photos of me.
... I'd thought Tianamen Square was big, but... Before it was a tourist attraction, the Forbidden City used to be like Buckingham Palace and the White House combined. For five hundred years, it was both the emperor's home, and the seat of the government. But unlike those single buildings in London and Washington, DC, the Forbidden City is spread out over 0.28 square miles, and houses 90 palaces and courtyards, with almost a thousand buildings in total. It is really more like a city inside the city. Seeing it all was going to prove...difficult. And, actually, as far as Fercho and I were concerned, not really necessary. The complex is divided into two parts, the Outer Court, which was for ceremonies, and the Inner Court, where the emperor lived. Twenty four different emperors lived there in all, from the Ming to the Qing dynasties.

Harmony was the order of the day, apparently, as there are halls (really, buildings) of Supreme Harmony, Central Harmony and Preserving Harmony. There is also a Hall of Mental Cultivation, one of Military Glory. Also, a Hall of Union, and I wondered if that was where the emperor had sex with his concubines. The buildings, the palaces, are gorgeous, of course, with their pagoda roofs and the golden carvings of dragons flanking the richly red walls, and the gilded lions at many entrance ways. But there are only so many thrones and intricately carved water spouts you can look at (and pose before) until, especially with my jet lag, they all begin to blur together. Yes, it's true, it was the ancient China I had dreamed of as a child, and here is was, towering before me, surrounding me, enveloping me. But there was mile after mile of it! I hadn't really gone there to see these sights; I was there to see Tina and Taal and to see the Wall. The Forbidden City was an interesting diversion. But not 980 buildings' worth. And the Underground City was waiting for me. Time was ticking by. I had to save some for that.

Fercho and I walked, talked, took photos, laughed a bit, and kept walking. We entered a palace, looked around in wonder, then exited. And then there was another. And another. And another. After hours of this, we reached a map and found the YOU ARE HERE dot. We were only a third of the way through. We had barely made a dent in the monstrosity that is the Forbidden City. And we still had to walk back.

I looked at Fercho. He looked at me. Who would be the first to say it?

"What do you think?" he asked.

"I think I've seen enough."

He deflated with relief.

"I'm glad you said that. Me, too."

"I've got other things to see besides this today," I said. "After this, I'm going to the Military Museum. And then the Underground City. That's what I'm really looking forward to. Hey, do you want to come with me?"

But he looked as doubtful at my choice of sightseeing destinations as Tina and Taal had.

"I've got to go to the Temple of Heaven." he said.

I guessed I'd have to pull my piece of paper out to get somebody to take photos of me for the rest of the trip.

"One last special photo, though," Fercho said.

He reached into his backpack and, to my surprise, pulled out a teddy bear.

"Believe it or not," he said, "I take a photo of myself with this bear wherever in the world I go. Would you do me the honor?"

And as I took the photo, a thought came to me. To this day I can't for the life of me comprehend why, but I had been hauling around a paperback copy of my first fiction book, *An Embarrassment of Riches*.

"Wow!" I said, handing him back his camera. "You've just given me an amazing idea! I wrote this book," I took it out, "and now I'm going to take photos of it everywhere I go, just like your bear. Even better, I'll get my friends and fans to take photos of themselves 'reading' the book when they go on vacation too!" And so a tradition was born.

After I had him pose with my book, we exchanged Facebook information, then back we walked. And walked. And walked. And said goodbye. I was glad I had met him. He was very nice. But that wasn't the last I'd see of him.

BEIJING AND THE GREAT WALL OF CHINA:

What was I thinking? Is this the effects of jet lag?

BEIJING AND THE GREAT WALL OF CHINA:

THE MILITARY MUSEUM OF THE CHINESE PEOPLE'S REVOLUTION

GERALD HANSEN

BEIJING AND THE GREAT WALL OF CHINA:

Located at 9 Fuxing Road (I kid you not), the Military Museum of the Chinese People's Revolution is not far from the Forbidden City. And thank God for that, because time was indeed flying by. It had taken us forever to walk back to the entrance of the Forbidden City. This would have to be a very quick visit to the museum if I was to make it to the Underground City as well.

As I approached the foreboding, Soviet-looking building that was the museum, it seemed a girls' middle school, or, given the amount of schoolgirls, more likely busloads of schools, had chosen it for a field trip/field trips. At least they were older than slit pants age.

What I had been expecting to be a rather masculine experience was softened by the giggling, skipping girls milling around me (and, of course, pushing past me and elbowing me). I had expected it to be a more historical museum, and, call me strange, but I've always had a thing for old missiles. And there were missiles aplenty. And also the first Chinese atomic bomb, and a few rooms about the space program, with satellites and an orbital capsule. There were many Soviet-style propaganda displays, which were also entertaining. They were done in exactly the same style, except the comrades, the workers, were Chinese.

When I entered the Hall of Weapons, however, it was like an NRA wet dream. The killing machines the People's Liberation Army used against their own people were proudly on display. Row after row of assault rifles and machine guns and other artillery. Tank after tank. They all looked modern, and were just horrible to look at, not entertaining or informative. A little Cultural Revolution, anyone? I was amazed that the girls were peering into the glass cases with interest and a giggle or two. I left, then looked up at the name of the next hall. To my shock, it was the Hall of the War to Resist US Aggression. It was apparently a showcase China's involvement in the Korean war. Head bowed, I scurried out.

BEIJING AND THE GREAT WALL OF CHINA:

THE SEARCH FOR
THE UNDERGROUND CITY

BEIJING AND THE GREAT WALL OF CHINA:

Now to enter the Underground City. All I needed to do was find Xidamochang Jie, wherever that was. I remembered from the guide book that, although the street was nowhere near Tianamen Square it was off a side street from it. There was a city map on the corner, and I tried to locate the street. In a megalopolis of a million streets. I stared and stared, ran my finger up and down all the streets that led off Tianamen Square. Chinese characters swam before my eyes. It was like a task they ask the contestants of *the Amazing Race* to do. Most main streets were listed in both Chinese and English, but not the smaller ones. After about twenty minutes, I finally verified that none of the larger streets leading off was this damn Xidamochang Jie.

There were plenty of people around me I could ask. If I could speak their language. But I did have my piece of paper. I pulled it out. "Where is…?" was one of the phrases. I could point to that, then …what? I didn't know how to 'spell' it in Chinese characters. All I had was the pinyin Xidamochang Jie.

I waved at a passing couple. "Ni hao!"
They ran away. I tried a businessman. "Ni hao!"
He scowled and marched down the sidewalk.
"Ni hao! Ni hao!"
I felt a tap on my shoulder, but this time it wasn't Fercho. It was an older man in a uniform. He held a broom in his hand.

He smiled rather unfortunate teeth, but he appeared friendly. A stream of Chinese erupted from his mouth, and I gathered he was asking what I wanted.

I looked at my paper and pointed to "Where is…?" Then I

pointed at a different paper that said Xidamochang Jie.

He actually scratched his head. Then he grabbed a woman with shopping who shrieked, but then listened as he babbled on. She turned to me. She smiled a marvelous smile. She looked at the letters that spelled the street name.

Then they talked on and on in front of me, at times nodding, at times shaking their head. Finally, the man grabbed the paper from me, and they approached another couple, and the four of them had what seemed like a heated discussion. All four went to the map, hands gestured, fingers pointed, and there was further discussion. The woman from the couple came up to me, and gestured 'under,' 'under.' I smiled and nodded. Yes! She knew I was after the Underground City! She trailed me over to the map, they all gabbled excitedly, and the woman with the shopping stabbed her finger at a street. There were murmurs of assent and nods of agreement. Then, beaming, Boy/Girl Scout duty for the day done, they slapped me on the back, the first man shook my hand, and they wandered off in three different directions.

I pulled out a pen and painstakingly wrote down the Chinese characters that was the street. It would be too difficult to find myself. I'd take a cab there. They were cheap. And all I had to do was show the driver the characters for Xidamochang Jie. I was relieved to see the street was short, because I had no number. But I assumed it would be easy to find the entrance to a tourist attraction.

I hailed a cab, there were plenty, and showed the driver my piece of paper. We drove for a while, and he pulled into a dingy, and therefore exciting, street. The fare was, of course, pennies. I got up, and wandered up the street, passing decaying hair salons (there are a multitude in Beijing), sketchy restaurants and the like. People spat in all directions around me. And then I wandered down the street. I didn't see anything that looked like the entrance to the Underground City. There should be a sign in English for it at least, I thought.

And then...I spied an archway with a banner above it. There were stone lions on either side. I had seen a photo of the entrance in the travel guide, and it had stone lions. My heart beat faster as I approached. This was it! I tugged at the door. It looked ancient and, yes, exciting. I tugged again. I tried to pull it. It seemed closed. But it was supposed to be open until 5:00, with last entrance at 4:15! It was only 4:00. The door was definitely locked. I knocked, then knocked more loudly. A man behind me laughed. I turned around, and he rattled off something in Chinese. He pointed to the right of the door, then walked off, shaking his head. There was a piece of paper plastered to the wall. It looked official. The headline was in Chinese and was red. At the bottom, there were a few words in English.

Undrgruond City close due renovation. Open soon. Kindly please wait.

It was dated September 2008. That was some long renovation.

I sighed. But, I considered, I had seen plenty enough that day, and most of it delightful. But those sights were only whetting my appetite for the main course. I couldn't get into the Underground City, but I still had the Great Wall ahead of me.

I went home. To pass out from exhaustion and jet lag.

By the way, it is now 2017, and the Underground City is still 'under renovation.' A very long renovation indeed.

BEIJING AND THE GREAT WALL OF CHINA:

HUTONGS AND WHAT NOT TO DO THERE

BEIJING AND THE GREAT WALL OF CHINA:

The hutongs are specific to Beijing and other large cities in Northern China. They are twisty alleyways formed by the walls of siheyuan, single family compounds with a sunny open courtyard in the middle where the children could play and granny could catch some rays. They were the gated communities of their day. I'm sure it was a delightful way to live. When the People's Republic was formed in 1949, the Chinese government demolished many of these siheyuan to make room for boulevards and high-rises. Those that escaped the bulldozer were divided up and offered to the masses, so that where one family used to live in splendor, many extended families now ate cheek to jowl, slept head to foot. Back in the day, the richer people lived closer to the Forbidden City (which was the center of Beijing), and so the siheyuans were more opulent there, less opulent farther away. Each siheyuan has an archway gate as an entrance (usually with a pagoda-type roof), and many have stone lions guarding the entrance. The buildings inside, the houses, are usually one story and gray, and the roofs are made of black slate. As time goes by, more and more have been destroyed to make way for supermarkets, theme parks, and probably mega Versace stores. Many lack modern conveniences, so maybe this is a good thing, but, of course, the charm of the past is being destroyed. The hutongs are the hidden hearts of the city.

On my second day, I went to the markets to get some cheap designer gear. It goes without saying you must bargain, and it's quite fun. The saleswomen, usually attractive, young perfect English speakers, are friendly and seem to love the haggling, the bit of vocal tennis. My favorite designer is Ben Sherman, and I had visions of hauling bulging suitcases packed with my new wardrobe back to New York. But they didn't sell any. There was Fred Perry, which is close, but I made do instead with Burberry. Probably fake Burberry, as the shirts I bought there still look brand new, no matter how many times I wash them.

I was heading back to the apartment. I had spent most of my cash in the market, and was wondering if I should begin the tiresome search for a Citibank ATM. On one side of the street there were endless rows of new high-rises, together with some quirky modern architectural wonders. I looked on the other side of the street. I stared.

Stone lions on either side of an ancient door. Both chipped, one without a head, but still. A warped door hanging off its hinges. A misshapen pagoda-type roof with broken and missing tiles. It was a hutong. A squalid, dilapidated hutong teetering precariously on crumbling bricks, to be sure. But a hutong nevertheless. I knew I had seen some on the map that were well-preserved and well-visited by tourists, but they were in a different part of the city. My heart raced. How I longed to enter that archway!

This seemed somewhere a tourist would fear to tread, maybe even dangerous for the people who lived there. But it was the old China not tainted by modernity. Could I just saunter in, camera slung around my neck, shopping bags packed with Burberry, and start popping off snapshots like ammo? Were these hutongs like the favelas of Rio, or the ghettos of Detroit? Would I be attacked, mugged, violated? A kidney ripped out of me? There seemed to be no crime in this city bristling with its freshly-ironed uniforms on every corner, but beyond that archway seemed like the underworld, the seething, seedy underbelly unknown to polite society. Rules that kept the rest of the city bound didn't seem to apply in this, the Wild West of the Far East. I craved excitement, yes, but it would take a braver soul than I to pass that archway into the past. This wasn't like the Underground City, where nobody lived, or indeed had lived. People probably lived here. It was their home. But what kind of people?

I started. A pedicab, sort of like a rickshaw, but with the driver on a bike, rattled up to me. The bike frame was rusty, the seat tattered and spattered with stains whose provenance I didn't want to consider. The bike was in a state of disrepair just like the hutong.

"Three! Three!" the man on the bike said. His face was dirty. So were his clothes. His eyes were bloodshot. Maybe he was drunk. He kept jabbing his finger at the entrance of the hutong. "Three! Three!"

He motioned for me to climb into the back of his pedicab.

"Tour! Tour!"

My fear was replaced by excitement. It was as if my prayers had been answered.

But I was surprised. Only three yuan? I put up three fingers. "Only three?" I asked. He nodded and his face broke out into what I gathered was a smile, showing what I supposed were teeth beyond. He held up three fingers. He seemed desperate. He seemed poor. His fingernails were filthy. Maybe, in his impoverished state, three yuan could buy him many things. Like more beer, perhaps. Still, I thought he probably meant thirty. That was fine. Forty five cents.

"Thirty?" I wondered. I counted it out on my hands.

He shook his head.

"Three!" he insisted. "Three!"

I shrugged. It was true that everything seemed dirt cheap in Beijing (at least on one side of every street), so maybe quite a lot could be bought with three yuan. Although it seemed too good to be true, I nodded and smiled.

"Hour!" he said.

Yes, I wanted to enter, yes, I wanted a tour, but I didn't want to bump around for an hour on that pedicab.

I shook my head. I motioned, "Half an hour."

"Hour!"

I felt bad, making him ride me around for an hour for three yuan. I shook my head.

"Half an hour," I said.

He muttered something, but finally seemed to agree. I climbed on. We teetered diagonally across the boulevard with speeding cars and trucks bearing down on us at all angles. I screamed. He turned around and smiled. Laughed.

He wheeled me through the archway. We entered a different China, a China of the past. The noise of the traffic outside faded away the deeper we traveled. I hid my shopping behind my back. I clutched the areas where I suspected kidneys were located as we bounced over rubble and debris and discarded household items. The houses here seriously looked about to collapse.

The hutong folk were hanging around just like they do in the shady parts of my neighborhood. As we whizzed through, I saw faces peering at us from cracked windows, faces fascinating in their exoticness, the faces of tribes from the time of Genghis Khan.

Dogs that looked feral barked and chased us, bit at the wheels of the pedicab. In some courtyard, a gang of men who, dare I say it, looked almost as feral were huddled around a fire, fanning the flames, smiling and pointing as we passed. Or were they laughing? Were they laughing at my driver? Me? The both of us? The state of his pedicab? It was difficult to know. Maybe smiling and laughing with us and at us at the same time.

On the safety of the sparkling, well-swept sidewalks outside, most people were decked out in all the best labels, hair professionally coiffed, strutting proudly towards their office jobs. All the people here seemed a bit wild; maybe it was their clothing. They seemed like drug addicts or problem drinkers, or maybe they had just lived long lives of hard labor, or perhaps even not that long. Maybe they had all been prematurely aged by too much work and too little shelter from the elements. Wind battered. They were living on the edge. On the edge of society, on the edge of the city, on the edge of the traditional and the modern.

It was thrilling. How I wish I had taken some photos, but I have a thing about photographing people I don't know. I feel like I'm objectifying them. So instead I snapped a few of the teetering buildings, the rubble, as we passed, though they didn't come out. The lighting was very bad there.

The tour came to an end. When the driver deposited me on the pavement outside back in modern Beijing proper, I climbed off. He unfolded a handwritten sign on a piece of tattered white cardboard. HUTONG TOUR it read. 300 yuan/15 minutes. 600 yuan/30 minutes. 1200 yuan/hour. He held out his hand.

"Three hundred?!" I gasped.

He nodded. He smiled. It was menacing.

"You said three! Three!"

He nodded and pointed at the sign.

"Three! Three!"

"Three hundred is not three!"

He got off his bike and towered over me.

"Three! Three!"

Panic gripped me. I looked wildly around, but that stretch of the sidewalk in the city of 21.5 million was strangely deserted. Perhaps the driver knew that. Still, was it a good idea or the worst idea to get the communist police involved? I was unregistered, after all. And maybe the Chinese would stick together. He had given me a service, and I wasn't paying. The amount he, with his cardboard, was plainly showing me. After the fact.

I reached into my pocket, scrabbled around and found a fifty yuan bill.

"That's all I have!" I said. Really, it was almost true.

A torrent of angry Chinese poured from his mouth. His fists rose in the air. I turned and ran down the sidewalk. I raced around a corner. I saw a subway. I clattered down the stairs. I leaned against the wall, shaking and catching my breath. I went home.

I know he was only trying to make a living. I felt guilty. Three hundred yuan wasn't much, after all. But he had said three, and I had figured on thirty. Maybe he really needed the money. Maybe he had children to feed. Though...thankfully, my guilt didn't have to extend to 'taking food out of his children's mouths,' as they are only allowed one. Or at least, back then they were, I think the one couple, one child regulation has been dropped since. So, at the very most, only one child would go hungry.

BEIJING AND THE GREAT WALL OF CHINA:

HOW TO FIND AN ENGLISH-SPEAKING CHINESE PERSON

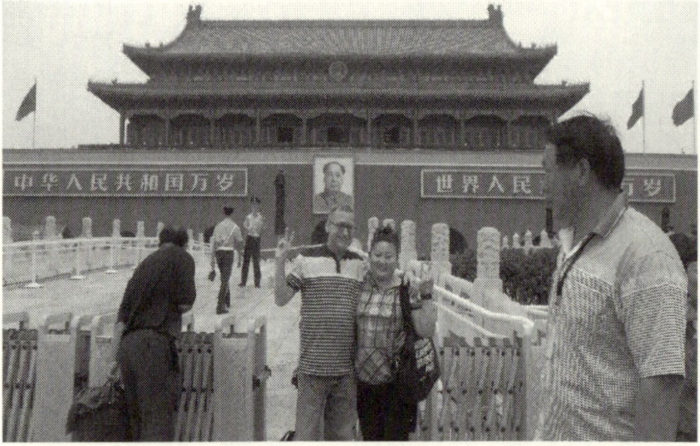
中华人民共和国万岁
世界人民
万岁

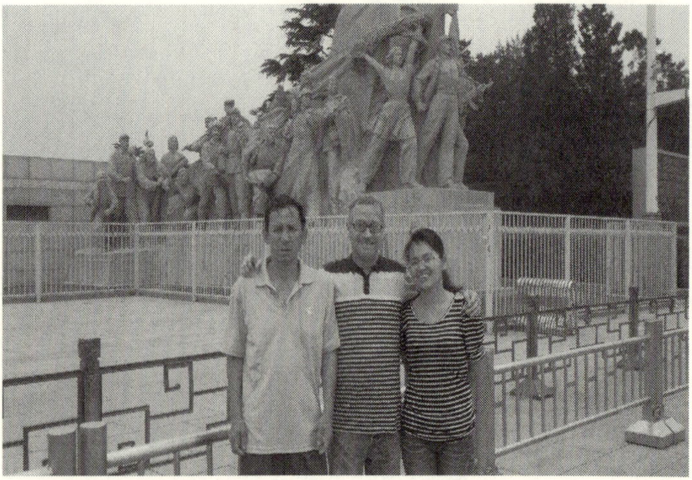

BEIJING AND THE GREAT WALL OF CHINA:

It's easier than you think. They find you.

In Beijing, the people who can speak English are few and far between, like needles in a field of haystacks. But when you come upon one, they are eager and excited to let you know. Of course, it's easy for them to tell you are probably an English speaker.

They spy you on the other side of a six lane boulevard, and gladly risk their lives, zigzagging, leaping through six lanes of heaving traffic just to say hello. As you are checking the city map, proud parents will suddenly push their teenage children at you and look on, beaming and nodding, as the kids rattle on in an English with an old-fashioned British accent. The parents and the children are equally excited, sometimes verging on too excited, at meeting a native speaker. They are thrilled at the chance to finally practice this strange language of the odd people from a far off land, a land that until recently it seemed about as likely they would visit as Mars.

Couples will ask you to pose for photographs with them. As you pose between them, you can feel them trembling with excitement. Really. And, of course, every encounter like this was a thrill for me too.

The conversation usually goes something like this:

"I beg your pardon. Nice to meet you, hello. Good afternoon. My name is X, and this is my betrothed X. Please kindly tell us your name."

"Please kindly tell what land you hail from."

"Please kindly arrange yourself with us for photography session."

or

"How do you do, kind sir? May we please have the pleasure

of conversing with you? Might I be so forward as to request you pose for a photograph with me and my wife and our relatives for the extreme pleasure of all? For fondness at a later date."

And after this, it's usually, "Please kindly, might I be so bold as to touch your arm hairs?"

The women love to touch your arm hair, and giggle and laugh while they do it. Like they are petting an alien animal. It's fun.

Outside these chance encounters on the street, in the markets selling designer? gear, all the saleswomen—and they do all seem to be women—speak perfect English. British English. I wonder if the government regularly inspects all the high school English classes, chooses the most attractive schoolgirls, and the best English speakers, then informs the parents their one child has been chosen to work in the market for tourists.

Regardless. After each of these conversations, I felt great. Everyone made me feel like a rock star everywhere I went.

BEIJING AND THE GREAT WALL OF CHINA:

STARTLING STREET FOOD AND FAKE EVERYTHING

BEIJING AND THE GREAT WALL OF CHINA:

At every restaurant on Tina's itinerary, we ate 'Chinese style," where many dishes are ordered, and everybody shares. This also seems to be Korean style and Taiwanese style. Tina did the ordering, and for that I'm grateful, as although some menus were also in English, is was broken English, and so difficult to understand what dish might actually be placed in front of you.

I couldn't help giggle at bit at eating Peking Duck in Beijing itself. Every time you order the dish, you have to reference a far flung city, but there I actually was, in 'Peking' itself. We ate it in a posh restaurant. The duck was prepared table side, and although that's something in a New York restaurant my wallet would be hard pressed to afford, in Beijing what looks like luxury dining is refreshingly cheap. A chef in a white hat rolled up the steaming duck (head and all), and set to work on it with his glinting, clacking knives. The hospital mask he was wearing didn't inspire confidence. Maybe he thought brown air might rise from it as he chopped into it? And chop he did. Chop! Chop! Chop! I flinched every time the knife hit the cutting board. But the duck was succulent and tasted gorgeous and seemed to be airborne-disease free.

The Shanghai restaurant's dinner was great also, but the highlight were the desserts, all made of shaved ice, each one a work of art. Tina ordered many to sample. It seems the Shanghai dessert style is sweet and sour mixed together. There were relatively regular flavors like mango and coconut. But some of them had odd ingredients like green beans, sweet potatoes and what are called 'glutinous rice balls.' I found them a bit challenging to my Western palate. They were eaten rather less vigorously, but, with so many to sample, we all waddled out, satisfied.

The highlight of Tina's restaurant itinerary for me, however, was the hot and spicy restaurant. But I mean mouth searing, sweat-pouring-down-your-beet-red-face hot and spicy. There's not much more mouthwatering to me than heaping mounds of chili peppers piled so high on plates that you need to use your chopsticks as drills or some industrial tool to burrow your way to the chunks of meat hidden underneath. Maybe that's some people's idea of dining hell, my it's my idea of heaven. Fat, plump peppers, slathered in a flesh-searing, mind-numbing sauce, dripping from whatever protein they were hiding, chicken, pork, cat, I didn't care; they were the extras. The chilies were the stars.

Speaking of food, in each country I go to, I love to check out the supermarkets. What flavors of soup do they have? What does their toothpaste look like? Call me strange, but a tube of foreign toothpaste is fascinating to me. I like to check out foreign necessities. A glance in the potato chip aisle is usually an eye opener, and Beijing was no exception. Of course, the packages were in Chinese, but there were helpful illustrations which let me know, to the slight heaving of my stomach, the flavors. Iced Tea with Lemon, Cucumber, Hot Pot, Blueberry, Hot and Sour Fish Soup. As for the other packaged food that lined the shelves, I remained a bit clueless, even with the illustrations and photos, usually with a smiling hostess with well-manicured nails indicating the item, as to what sustenance (allegedly) might be contained within.

In street markets, I checked out a vegetable stand, or maybe it was a fruit stand. In some countries, it's difficult to tell what are vegetables and what are fruit. On display were 30 shades of brown, oddly shaped tubular growths with roots snaking out at odd angles. I couldn't imagine any of it as food.

But now, dear friend, I will take you on a little journey where only the brave and iron-stomached should tread, a trip to the street food vendors. They line every sidewalk at random. This is on the 'old' side of the streets. There aren't really stalls as such, just a table or maybe even a cardboard box somebody has lugged from somewhere and plunked down wherever there was space. They are everywhere, so they're difficult to avoid.

Maybe you've heard the rumors, and, yes, they're true. A glance at most Beijing food stalls would make your hunger flee. I peered over to see what was on offer. It was as if shards of glass were pricking my brain. My stomach heaved.

What would I like to nibble on? A grilled scorpion on a stick? Or perhaps one of the wide array of speared beetles? No, thanks. How about a spoonful of deep fried silkworm cocoons? Oh! And what are these delights flattened like a flying rat? With their twig-like legs and little claws at the end? Lizards? And this serving of fish heads? Though tradition has it that the eyes will make you see better and the brains, tiny gelatin-like things, will make you smarter, I'll pass.

I hear the government is cracking down on the street food vendors, and that's a shame. Because all around me, even as my own stomach clenched with horror, people were eagerly buying everything and happily chomping into it. And, of course, everything cost pennies.

There are also restaurants that cater to the more esoteric of Chinese tastes. Leaving aside for the moment the dog hotpot and pig brain hotpot and sheep spinal cord hotpot, the most horrifying, I think (though feminists may disagree) is the penis hotpot, featuring the tackle of a variety of your most beloved furry creatures, sheep, deer, donkey, horse and, of course, dog. Snake penises are thrown in there as well, for extra 'virility,' as every snake has two. You can wash it down with a snifter of delicious duck blood.

Yes, I am a bit adventurous, I love excitement, but—come on! There are limits!

Is it any wonder I scurried to the safety of McDonalds on the swanky side of the street? Once I had located a real one. As anyone who has ordered, let's say, Sephora from Amazon, from the Marketplace, not from Amazon itself, can tell you, there's a moment when you eagerly open the package that has arrived, and then your heart falls. You discover to your dismay it has been shipped from China, and you know what that means. Fake.

Many US cities have a Chinatown, and if they are anything like New York's Chinatown (we actually have three, one in Manhattan, Brooklyn and Queens), if you go shopping there, you know the Chinese are experts at replication. A switch and bait, you are shown an 'original' Louis Vuitton satchel, only to get it home and the one in your (plastic shopping) bag reveals itself to be a Loui Vutton. There are fake IDs, fake Burberry scarves, fake Calvin Klein One, fake iPhones and tablets. Similarly, in China itself, there is a fake Disneyland (the ears of Mickey Mouse just different enough to stop lawsuits, or maybe Disney has tried, but the distance too far and the Chinese lawyers too good), fake Lamborghinis, and a fake Pentagon. There is also a fake, life-sized Leaning Tower of Pisa and a fake Taj Mahal.

There are also fake McDonalds. You can usually tell because the 'M' is either upside down or double, like MM, but connected. Just like there are fake Starbucks. You spy the familiar logo and your excitement is tempered as you get closer and realize the mermaid has only one eye or an extra arm. You realize it's a Sunbucks, a Starbox, a Star & Bucks, a USABucks or even a Starfucks (really!). On Tina's block, there was a Pizza Huh, a 7-12, and a OFC (that last one had the Colonel's face).

So at the food stalls, I'd lost my nerve, but not my appetite. I was still ravenous. So I fled. And, to my shame, I fled to McDonalds.

Yes, I know, I know. It's the most horrible thing in the world to do, eat at McDonald's in a foreign country. But if you had seen youself the things on the sticks, some of them still wriggling, you might have raced to the golden arches yourself. And been grateful for cultural empiricism. I was faced with two choices: be a wimpy bad tourist, or starve.

And, I'm embarrassed to say, Starbucks was my other refuge, if only for their free wi-fi. Maybe there was free wi-fi elsewhere, but with everything in Chinese, how would I ever know?

Though I must say this, going to a Chinese McDonald's (or a Russian or Japanese one, for that matter) is an experience in itself. The overhead menus are never in English, and although it's easy to detect the Big Mac and the Chicken McNuggets from the photos, there are always intriguing new items geared towards the indigenous taste. So even eating in McDonald's can be exotic and different. And it's interesting to note that, in most countries, there are security guards posted outside. I wonder about the executive decision made at some global McDonald's board meeting where they were deemed necessary: "American tourists are by nature terrified, and we must post security guards outside each one in the less American parts of the world so they feel safe buying Happy

Meals for their children." or "American tourists will flock to McDonalds worldwide, and we want them to feel safe," or "We somehow think that McDonald's are more likely to be raided than other stores in your countries, so you must post security guards there."

BEIJING AND THE GREAT WALL OF CHINA:

THE WALL

GERALD HANSEN

BEIJING AND THE GREAT WALL OF CHINA:

I awoke the third morning, still muddled with jet lag but thrilled. Tina and I were going to the Great Wall! Taal had to work (though maybe he was a bit relieved not to have to accompany us). I looked out the bedroom window and smiled. It was Blue Sky Day. It boded well for our trip. Tina had told me we were going to the section of the wall called Badaling. It was the closest to Beijing, she'd told me, and also the most popular. Cheng would take us there.

I think everyone knows the Great Wall was built over centuries to keep the northern border of China safe from marauding hoards. As early as the 7th century, small walls were being built. They were probably made out of earth and wood. But the wall we all think of, that majestic monster built of stone and brick, with signal towers for surveillance and parapets for shooting the invaders, was constructed mainly during the Ming dynasty. That dynasty lasted for centuries, from the 1300s to the 1600s.

The Great Wall is in fact many walls cobbled together, and in some stretches not connected at all. This is why it is so difficult for there to be an official length. It's over 5000 miles long, though. Some sections are better preserved, better connected and more photogenic than others. How someone could walk the entire length, I don't know. There must be sections where they need a helicopter to get from one wall to the other. In some areas, especially in the West, the Wall is anything but majestic, more mounds of dirt.

Oh, and it can't been seen from space, but it is true that if you piled all the sections atop one another, it would reach the moon. It can't even be seen in orbit, as some think, and certainly not from the moon. (They asked Neil Armstrong, and he said no.)

I can only imagine Tina's fixed grin when I had told her on the phone that the one thing I wanted to see when I visited was the Great Wall. Every friend visiting New York wants to see the Empire State Building, and although you roll your eyes at going there again, it's just a short subway ride away, and there it is, towering above you. To get to the Wall is a journey. Badaling is a two-hour drive from Beijing. And for a reason that will eventually be revealed, Tina and I made that journey to the Wall again a few years later. But both times, she shared my excitement at going. She's a good friend and a good sport, and for that I'm grateful.

We piled into the car, bottles of water and provisions in hand. We chatted and laughed as the car zigzagged through the exhaust fumes of the pulsating traffic and forced its way through Beijing, heading north and out of the city. Everywhere I looked, I saw buildings under construction. And not townhouses or five story apartments, but massive, scary tenement-looking monstrosities that seemed impossible to fill, even taking China's population into account.

But, in a country were everyone must have a job, I suppose they may as well construct buildings, whether they can fill them or not.

As we rode, the cafe called, then one restaurant, then the other. Tina blathered on in Chinese, a wide array of emotions in her voice. The problems seemed to be many and varied and, as she continued to talk down the line as the miles flew by, incredibly complicated. I felt a bit guilty taking Tina away from her work, but maybe she was relieved not to be there. The managers could deal with the immediate problems. Which is what she told me when, eventually, she hung up.

We hadn't even gone to the Wall yet, hadn't even planned how we might get down, and already I was looking forward to being back in New York and showing off the photos of myself posing on the world wonder, the first on the New7Wonders list I would visit. With the uncertainties and unknowns already behind me, the money spent and the trip over, and my camera bulging with amazing photos of myself and perhaps Tina too, draped across the wall in various poses.

Photos of a childhood dream that would prove it had come true, and those photos would continue to exist even as I got older and older and my memory of the event ever hazier.

As Tina had talked on the phone, we passed the Olympic stadium, official name the Beijing National Stadium, but known more commonly by its shape as the Bird's Nest. Then we had left Beijing, and soon, out the window, I saw in the horizon those mountains of the childhood wall hangings. The funky, jagged curves, the craggy mountaintops that scream 'only in China.' I was getting more and more excited.

And finally we were there. Cheng parked, and Tina had a little discussion with him. "He's going to pick us up in three hours. Is that good for you?"

"Sure," I said.

We gathered our belongings, and it was then I discovered I'd left my camera back at the apartment. And my phone. "Don't worry,"

Tina comforted, "I've got my phone. We can take photos with that."

She looked down at it. "Hmm, not much battery left, but we should be okay. Let's go. We've got to take a cable car up."

Looking up, I could see the Wall snaking around the mountain, the mountains. Little dots that I assumed were people scrabbled up and down the length of it. We would soon be two of those dots ourselves. I was bubbling with excitement.

Getting up to the Wall is a blast in itself, but taking a cable car to get there makes it even more of one. You already know what getting the tickets was probably like, so I'll skip that, and just say that, again, the entrance to the Wall and the cable car up is incredibly cheap.

I hooted with delight on our way up. Tina joined in. What an experience, and to share it with one of my best friends in the world, priceless, as the ads say. The view was breathtaking.

I'm not joking, when the cable car deposited us in the heart of the Great Wall, as we actually stood there *on it,* as it spread out in all its majesty before us, behind us, towered over us, as we could *touch* its magnitude, my knees were weak. I was giddy. The sun was beating down on us, but I didn't care (Tina less so, I imagine). All I cared about was being on the Wall.

When you take these trips in your mind, sometimes reality matches your imagination. Sometimes there are unexpected factors that make it slightly different to how you imaged it.

That day just happened to be, to our chagrin, some school holiday, and the walls were crawling with tens, no, hundreds, of toddlers (many in the dreaded slit-pants), children, tweens, mothers with infants strapped to them. Pushing, shoving, spitting.

"I thought they were only allowed one child per family?" I asked. Tina had no answer.

Indeed, on this stretch of the wall it seemed the government had given these families free reign to birth babies once every nine months. We could see just how many families there were in China. Style for the children of the day seemed to be knitted caps (even in the heat) with animal ears, pandas and cheetahs and I don't know what. Those pushing past our knees all seemed to be wearing them. But we would deal with the children the best way we could, by ignoring them. It wasn't to be. As we stared about us, wondering if we should go up that hill or down that way, we heard children screaming, shouting. Saw them pointing. At us.

The Chinese may be many things, industrious, pragmatic, spiritual, for example, but tall and blonde are two they usually aren't. I am blond and Tina is tall. And African-American, a third thing the Chinese aren't.

As we climbed the Wall (we decided to walk up) some children snickered, some howled with laughter, some shrieked and jumped up and down in uncontrollable excitement, fingers jabbing the air in our direction at our otherworldliness. Others fled, seemingly in fear, to the closest

BEIJING AND THE GREAT WALL OF CHINA:

Chinese adult for cover, clamping their little arms around the adults' legs. Some ran up and touched us, as if to verify our existence, as if we were suddenly sighted unicorns, myths only heard of from grandmothers' lips magically materializing in the flesh before them. Which, to some of them, we probably were. Later, Cheng explained to us that most of those children would have come from the 'outer provinces' and that, indeed, we were probably the first (a) black and (b) white people they had ever seen. And both together? What a spectacle in their young marveled minds! They would go back to their provincial villages, Cheng was sure, and talk more about the creatures they had encountered (Tina and I) than the Wall itself.

It is slippery. It is steep. There are no handrails. They are the furthest thing from wheelchair accessible it is possible to be. Back in the day when the Wall was built, the many centuries that that spanned, there was apparently no standardization of Wall step sizes, as one tiny step is followed by a mammoth one where legs are not enough to step up. Hands must grapple the next step and you sort of haul yourself up, then mince up the next tiny three steps, then haul yourself up the following giant four, and so on. And grappling them is difficult, as they are so slippery.

Where there are no steps to maneuver, when it stretches before you in a slanting ramp you fear has no end, there is still the slickness to contend with. You must tread very, very carefully. Thankfully, it wasn't raining, but I can only imagine, if it were the US, the lawsuits that would clog up the courts for decades. There is no such lawsuit culture in China, apparently, as all around us, there were squeals and shrieks as kids/brats and adults alike slid across the slabs and collided with parts of the wall or each other. Hands lunged toward the closest stranger for support and/or balance. If I'm making this sound like a nightmare, I don't mean to. It was hilarious, and the shrieking was usually followed by hoots of laughter, though some of it nervous.

As we huffed and puffed our way up the Wall, watchtowers loomed over us at regular intervals, and they were cool and damp inside. Also, along the sides, there are small rooms that were used for who only knows what, probably something military. As we passed, I peered inside a few, looking for evidence of binge drinking or unauthorized sex, but I couldn't detect anything. But they were great places to peer through the centuries-old 'windows' and luxuriate in the scenery. Like I said before, the Wall is one place where you get two for the price of one. A New7Wonder and wonderful scenery together. It truly is magical.

Other sections of the wall, strangely, just peter out into piles of rubble, and you have to turn around and take another route. It was on one of these sections we decided to pose for photos. (The photos here so far are from our second trip a few years later, if you were wondering.)

I posed with children bumping into my shins, chased them away, then posed again. Tina posed, 'reading' my book. Then we motioned and gestured for a passing woman to take our photo. We arranged ourselves as best we could, trying to find our footing, as that part of the wall was slanting.

"We'll get better ones later," Tina whispered. We smiled, the woman took two photos, then handed back Tina's camera. Then the battery died. That was it. Four measly photos. Not even a full five. Four. Perhaps, though, it was a blessing, as we then had to look at the Wall with our eyes, and experience it that way, instead of through a little hole on a lens. But, still.

The above photo is one of the Four. A few years later, Tina called and asked if I wanted to come visit again. I had already experienced Beijing, had already been to the Wall, and there were other, new places in the world I had yet to explore. But I wanted to see Tina and Taal again. And I only had four photos. "Sure," I said. "But...I hate to say it...we have to go back to the Wall. To get more photos."

She laughed and agreed wholeheartedly. What a trooper. And then, having thought a bit about the Chinese and their reputation for making 'replications,' I looked closely at those four old photos. I noticed that the bricks didn't seem centuries old. But perhaps they had just been cleaned. Or maybe they were in a state of disrepair and had been recently repaired to prevent more slips and falls. Why does that section seem to lead nowhere? Is it just me, I wondered, or could Tina and I have visited the most disappointing fake in that entire country? A fake Great Wall? Is it, in fact, just a wall?

It turns out that the Badaling section had been 'extensively renovated' before opening to the public, to the millions of Beijing in particular, as a tourist destination. This was in 1957, so it was for the benefit of Chinese tourists, as foreign ones, especially capitalist Americans, must have been far and few between, if nonexistent, back then. As I look at the photo now, that mortar doesn't seem ancient. Had Tina and I just gone, not to the Great Wall of China, but just to a wall in China?

Perhaps there was a government incentive to keep more people employed. Mission: build fake Wall sections and age them. Who knows if we actually went to a 'real' part of the Wall. But the second time we went to Mutiyanu, which is further away from Beijing and less crowded (and there were few children), so at least we hedged out bets.

It's difficult to know if renovation really leads to replacement. How much needs to be destroyed to spruce something up a bit?

The Pyramids are old, and they look old. But there are other ancient sites, like Chichén Itzá, that have been spruced up a bit (too spruced up, if you ask me; who wants to see a pristine 1000 year old monument? I want my dirt, I want my crumbling bricks and dust.) I do understand the need for renovation, however. And I am grateful that Badaling's Wall (or wall) shows the glory of the Wonder. It isn't the same along all 5000-plus miles of the Wall There are stories of far flung sections of the Wall to the West, where village children use it as a playground, and it is covered with graffiti and strewn with garbage. Many miles of the Wall seem to have 'disappeared' recently. Bricks are stolen to build other buildings, or to sold on eBay.

Cheng would be waiting for us. It was time for us to make our way down. "How do you want to get down?" Tina asked.

"I have a choice?"

"Do you want to hike it?"

Apparently, hiking down was a 'done thing' by some people. Maybe crazy people.

"Absolutely not."

She deflated with relief.

"We have three other ways to get down. We can take the cable car again. Or there's a bobsled. Some people enjoy it." She said this lightly, but her face had an odd grin. Her left eye twitched. A look at her let me know we shouldn't choose this option, had I even wanted to, which I didn't.

"And the last?"

Her face collapsed with relief, and the twitch fled. This just shows what a great friend she is, giving me every available option and the grace of letting me choose. If it had been me, I would've left out the 'hiking' option.

"Or we can take a bobsled-rollercoaster type thing."

"A—?"

Yes, a bobsled-rollercoaster type thing.

A small fee and ten minutes later, I found myself sat in a rather wobbly contraption that didn't inspire much confidence I would get to the parking lot alive. Tina was ahead of me. She turned around, a face like she was about to give birth to triplets. The bobsled started, whizzing down the mountain. My terrified eyes caught sight of yellow metal fences on the areas where you might fling out of it and go toppling over the edge. I clutched onto the rail for dear life. It took a mere four minutes, and they whizzed by like an eternity. We were greeted at the bottom by men dressed as Chinese warriors who you can pose with for a smaller fee. And souvenirs.

I bought a few Little Red Books and some Chairman Mao key chains. We headed to the parking lot, and looked around for the car. Tina's phone, of course, was dead, so we couldn't call Chang.

And as we waited, and as we reflected on the amazement of what we had just seen, and on the danger our lives had just been in on the way down, we heard, echoing across the parking lot and through those oh-so-Chinese-mountains, "Gerald! Gerald!"

Tina turned to me, eyes agog.

"Who in the name of God do you know...? Here at the Great Wall?"

My jaw had also dropped. But it was Fercho, swaggering towards us.

"You're here, too?"

What a small world, indeed!

Years later, I visited Fercho in Bogotá, and his brother and mother, and I had a great time. But that's another story, and another book.

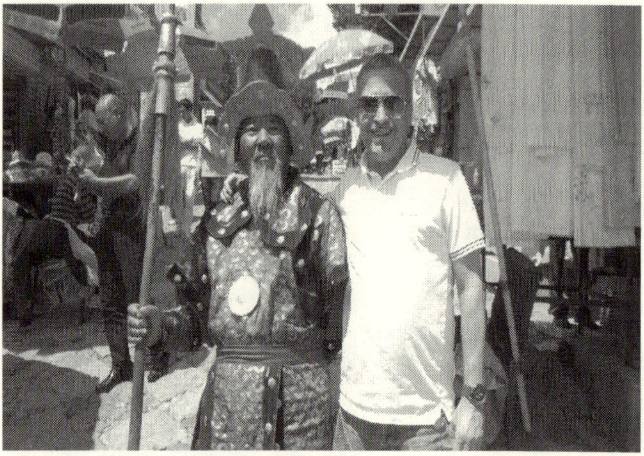

BEIJING AND THE GREAT WALL OF CHINA:

A FEW THOUGHTS

Maybe this is an elephant in the room I haven't addressed, and maybe you are wondering if PC kept me from mentioning it. No, I was waiting until now. Anyone who knows me knows I steer clear of PC. If you are easily offended, please don't read further. But here's what I have to say: I don't know why people think Asians look alike. Everyone's an individual, of course, and while it's true that a few Japanese, for example, might look more Korean, a few Taiwanese might be mistaken for Thai, in general, especially after teaching ESL for so long, it's easy for me to tell the difference at a glance. In Beijing, I was interesting how *different* everyone looked. There were different types of Chinese, and it was very easy to see.

The Russian Federation is free, but still seems repressive and communist, people terrified of the police these days instead of the KGB (though this has to do with corruption and their greed for bribes. It seems they aren't in the job to serve the public, but instead for their their bank accounts and vacations to the Maldives.) Alternatively, the People's Republic of China is communist, but seems capitalist. Well, except for the blocking of Facebook and YouTube, the leaf-raking uniforms, the strange guest registration process and the fear of breaking the law it invokes if you (a) do it or (b) don't do it. There's a carefree atmosphere in the air among all the chaos, a delicateness in the people. A delicateness at odds with the military power, of course, but if I had to choose to spend my life in democratic Russia or communist China, I know where I'd choose. (Sorry to all my Russian friends about that; I know you are great, but...)

Here's what I think: wherever you go, you bring yourself with you. (I lived in Keflavik, Iceland on the edge of a barren, treeless lava field for three years and had a blast). Once, when I wrote on Facebook that I was going to some country, a 'friend' I had known decades ago messaged me something like, "X is a dirty, filthy place filled with disgusting people. You will get robbed and bla bla bla" he ranted on. I replied to him, "You said this before I went to another country, and you were wrong. So I tend to doubt you this time. Maybe the problem with every country you visit is that you were there." He unfriended me, of course, and I guess I was happy about that. But I think you get the point.

You should travel our wonderful without fear. Those who fear something always seem to confront it. The only person I've known who seemed scared by credit card fraud was in fact the only person whose identity was every stolen online. It seems, similarly, that those who envisioned lands without toilet paper were greeted with the horror of an empty holder hanging on the wall beside them. They were unfortunate enough to head for the stall the day the person whose government mandated job it was to stock the toilet paper had called in sick. Those who fear mosquito bites always seem to get bitten. I never do. But maybe it's because they don't like my blood.

Similarly, ISIS is threatening to blow up the Pyramids and the Hagia Sophia and the Taj Mahal. Well, yes. But aren't they threatening to blow up the entire world? So of course the

Pyramids and the Hagia Sophia and the Taj Mahal are included. Probably they've included the Great Wall also. Threatening isn't doing. On the news, I've noticed that with every attack of somebody on someone else, terrorism first has to be ruled out. When it was a knife wielding lunatic on a lone stretch of highway in the middle of nowhere, why was terrorism even considered in the first place? That mindset means the terrorists are winning. Why live in fear? Actually, having my kidney stolen is more likely, as far as I'm concerned. And the likelihood of that is unlikely. But, still, I'd better race to get to my last two New7Wonders, the Taj Mahal and Petra, before they are blown up!

I thank you so much for getting this book. If you enjoyed it (and I hope you did!), why not review it on Amazon? I don't even mean a review; many people don't like to write them. Really what's important are the stars, so even a sentence would do. Reviews/stars are so, so important for us authors, and we are always grateful for them. I'd love to hear from you!

TABLE FOR NINE AT KEBABALICIOUS

✯ ✯ ✯

A SHORT STORY

✯ **GERALD HANSEN** ✯

And keep in touch with all my activities, freebies and special offers! Sign up for my mailing list And if you do—how exciting!—you'll get my new short story, Table For Nine At Kebabaliciouss, from my fiction series The Irish Lottery Series, just for signing up at http://eepurl.com/cKqMYD

In the meantime, Jet Lag Jerry has booked a flight for his next trip to another modern world wonder. This time, Peru and Machu Picchu. Coming soon!

Made in the USA
Columbia, SC
18 February 2018